MY INSTANT POT

2022

DELICIOUS AND EASY TO MAKE RECIPES

JAMES SMITH

Table of Contents

Crunchy Mushrooms 10

Wrapped Shrimp 12

Lentils Spread 14

Paprika Cranberry Dip 15

Citrus Onion Spread 16

Zucchini and Squash Dip 17

Garlic Cauliflower Dip 19

Broccoli Spread 21

Cumin Cheese Spread 22

Leeks and Bell Pepper Spread 24

Chicken, Spinach and Avocado Salad 26

Pesto Barley Bowls 27

Balsamic Olives Salsa 28

Cheese Dip with Peppers 29

Juicy Chicken Drumettes 30

Creamy Cauliflower Bites 31

Yummy Baby Carrots 33

Cheesy Keto Dip 34

Simple Brussels Sprouts 36

Quick Spinach Dip 37

Asparagus with Mayo Dip 38

Keto Greens Dip 39

Cocktail Sausages Asian-Style 41

Stuffed Mushrooms with Cheese 43

Family Meatballs 45

Fresh Keto Meatballs 47

Preparation Time: 20 minutes 49

Delicious Cauliflower Tots 51

Keto Broccoli Balls 53

Cheesy Taco Dip 54

Meatballs with Cheese 56

Spanish Fat Bombs 58

Yummy Cocktail Wieners 60

Fresh Brussels Sprouts with Aioli Sauce 62

Cheesy Bacon Bites 63

Juicy Meatballs 65

Perfect Chicken Wings 67

2-Ingredients Chicken Wings 69

Sticky Chicken Wings 71

Simple Boiled Peanuts 73

Southern Boiled Peanuts 75

Hard Boiled Eggs 77

Steamed Artichokes 78

Zingy Boiled Peanuts 80

Unique Party Food	82
Decadent Liver Pâté	84
Exotic Mushroom Pâté	86
Garden Fresh Salsa	88
Party Meatballs	90
Cheese Loaded Burgers	92
Mini Sausage Bites	94
Refreshing Curd	96
The Best Jam Ever	97
Divine Pears	98
Berry Marmalade	99
Orange Delight	100
Simple Squash Pie	101
Winter Pudding	103
Banana Dessert	105
Apple Cake	107
Special Vanilla Dessert	109
Tasty and Amazing Pear Dessert	110
Cranberries Jam	111
Lemon Jam	112
Special Dessert	113
Superb Banana Dessert	114
Rhubarb Dessert	115
Plum Delight	116

Refreshing Fruits Dish	117
Dessert Stew	118
Original Fruits Dessert	119
Delicious Apples and Cinnamon	120
Crazy Delicious Pudding	121
Wonderful Berry Pudding	123
Winter Fruits Dessert	125
Different Dessert	126
Orange Dessert	127
Great Pumpkin Dessert	129
Delicious Baked Apples	131
Moist Pumpkin Brownie	133
Lemon Custard	135
Pumpkin Pudding	137
Easy Yogurt Custard	139
Zucchini Pudding	141
Delicious Pina Colada	142
Apple Caramel Cake	143
Apple Rice Pudding	144
Vegan Coconut Risotto Pudding	145
Vanilla Avocado Pudding	146
Vanilla Almond Risotto	148
Coconut Raspberry Curd	149
Simple Chocolate Mousse	151

The Best Tropical Dessert Ever	153
Crème with Almond and Chocolate	155
Cinnamon Flan	157
Yummy Upside-Down Cake	159
Extraordinary Chocolate Cheesecake	161
Old-School Cheesecake	163
Sweet and Sour Tale Cake	165
Lazy Sunday Cake	167
Keto Chocolate Brownies	169
Sweet Porridge with a Twist	171
Cheesecake Tropicana	172
Classic Holiday Custard	174
Blackberry Espresso Brownies	176
Sweet Porridge with Blueberries	178
Vanilla Berry Cupcakes	180
Mini Cheesecakes with Berries	182
Special Berry Crisp with Cinnamon	184
Yummy Fire Cheesecake	186
Classic Carrot Cake	188
Classic Brownie with Blackberry-Goat Cheese Swirl	190
Special Birthday Cake	193
Holiday Blueberry Pudding	195
Fluffy Strawberry Cake	197
Chocolate Cheesecake	200

Raspberry Compote 202

Chocolate Cream 204

Butter Pancakes 206

Lemon Cupcakes with Blueberries 208

Chocolate Brownies 210

Peach Pie 212

Almond Butter Cookies 214

Mini Brownie Cakes 216

Crunchy Mushrooms

Preparation Time: 10 minutes

Servings 4

Nutritional Values per serving: 91 Calories; 6.4g Fat; 5.5g Total Carbs; 5.2g Protein; 2.8g Sugars

Ingredients

- 2 tablespoons butter, melted
- 20 ounces button mushrooms, brushed clean
- 2 cloves garlic, minced
- 1 teaspoon dried basil
- 1 teaspoon dried rosemary
- 1 teaspoon dried sage
- 1 bay leaf
- Sea salt, to taste
- 1/2 teaspoon freshly ground black pepper
- 1/2 cup water
- 1/2 cup broth, preferably homemade
- 1 tablespoon soy sauce
- 1 tablespoon fresh parsley leaves, roughly chopped

Directions

1. Press the "Sauté" button to heat up your Instant Pot. Once hot, melt the butter and sauté the mushrooms and garlic until aromatic.

2. Add seasonings, water, and broth. Add garlic, oregano, mushrooms, thyme, basil, bay leaves, veggie broth, and salt and pepper to your instant pot.
3. Secure the lid. Choose "Manual" mode and High pressure; cook for 5 minutes. Once cooking is complete, use a quick pressure release; carefully remove the lid.
4. Arrange your mushrooms on a serving platter and serve with cocktail sticks. Bon appétit!

Wrapped Shrimp

Preparation time: 5 minutes

Cooking time: 6 minutes

Servings: 4

Ingredients:

1 pound shrimp, peeled and deveined

1 cup tomato sauce

A drizzle of olive oil

8 ounces bacon slices

1 teaspoon chili powder

A pinch of salt and black pepper

Directions:

1. In a bowl, mix the shrimp with the oil, salt, pepper and chili powder and toss.
2. Set the instant pot on Sauté mode, add the shrimp and cook for 2 minutes.
3. Transfer the shrimp to a bowl, cool it down and wrap each in a bacon slice.
4. Put the tomato sauce in your instant pot, arrange wrapper shrimp inside, put the lid on and cook on High for 4 minutes.
5. Release the pressure fast for 5 minutes, arrange the shrimp on a platter and serve.

Nutritional Values per serving: Calories 162, fat 3, fiber 4, carbs 7, protein 6

Lentils Spread

Preparation time: 10 minutes

Cooking time: 20 minutes

Servings: 6

Ingredients:

- 20 ounces tomatoes, crushed
- 3 garlic cloves, minced
- 1 and ½ cups red lentils, rinsed
- A pinch of salt and black pepper
- 1 tablespoon chives, chopped
- 1 tablespoon lemon juice
- 1 and ½ cups low-sodium veggie stock

Directions:

1. In your instant pot, mix the tomatoes with the lentils, salt, pepper and the stock, put the lid on and cook on High for 20 minutes.
2. Release the pressure naturally for 10 minutes, transfer the lentils mix to a food processor, add the rest of the ingredients except the chives, pulse well, divide into small bowls, sprinkle the chives on top and serve.

Nutritional Values per serving: Calories 167, fat 4, fiber 3, carbs 8, protein 6

Paprika Cranberry Dip

Preparation time: 6 minutes

Cooking time: 15 minutes

Servings: 4

Ingredients:

- 2 and ½ teaspoons lemon zest, grated
- 1 teaspoon chili powder
- 1 teaspoon sweet paprika
- 12 ounces cranberries
- ¼ cup orange juice

Directions:

1. In your instant pot, combine all the ingredients, put the lid on and cook on High for 15 minutes.
2. Release the pressure fast for 6 minutes, blend the mix using an immersion blender, divide into bowls and serve as a dip.

Nutritional Values per serving: Calories 141, fat 2, fiber 4, carbs 5, protein 4

Citrus Onion Spread

Preparation time: 5 minutes

Cooking time: 7 minutes.

Servings: 4

Ingredients:

- 1 cup cream cheese, soft
- A pinch of salt and black pepper
- 1 tablespoon olive oil
- 6 spring onions, chopped
- Juice of 1 orange
- 1 cup water

Directions:

1. In a bowl, combine the cream cheese with spring onions and the rest of the ingredients except the water, whisk well and transfer to a ramekin.
2. Add the water in the instant pot, add the trivet inside, place the ramekin in the pot, put the lid on and cook on Low for 7 minutes.
3. Release the pressure fast for 5 minutes and serve the spread right away.

Nutritional Values per serving: Calories 120, fat 2, fiber 3, carbs 5, protein 4

Zucchini and Squash Dip

Preparation time: 5 minutes

Cooking time: 15 minutes

Servings: 4

Ingredients:

- 1 yellow onion, chopped
- 1 tablespoon olive oil
- 1 and ½ pounds zucchini, chopped
- 1 butternut squash, peeled and roughly chopped
- ½ cup veggie stock
- 1 tablespoon lemon juice
- 1 tablespoon basil, chopped
- 2 garlic cloves, minced
- 1 tablespoon mint, chopped

Directions:

1. Set your instant pot on Sauté mode, add the oil, heat it up, add the onion and garlic, stir and cook 4 minutes.
2. Add zucchinis and the rest of the ingredients except the basil and the mint, put the lid on and cook on High for 10 minutes.
3. Release the pressure fast for 5 minutes, blend the mix using an immersion blender, divide into bowls and serve with mint and basil sprinkled on top.

Nutritional Values per serving: Calories 170, fat 5, fiber 3, carbs 4, protein 6

Garlic Cauliflower Dip

Preparation time: 10 minutes

Cooking time: 15 minutes

Servings: 4

Ingredients:

- 1 yellow onion, chopped
- 1 tablespoon olive oil
- A pinch of salt and black pepper
- 1 tablespoon rosemary, chopped
- 3 garlic cloves, minced
- ½ cup chicken stock
- 1 pound cauliflower florets
- ½ cup coconut cream
- 1 tablespoons parsley, chopped

Directions:

1. Set your instant pot on Sauté mode, add the oil, heat it up, add the onion, stir and cook for 5 minutes.
2. Add the rest of the ingredients except the cream and parsley, put the lid on and cook on High for 10 minutes.
3. Release the pressure naturally for 10 minutes, add the cream, blend the mix using an immersion blender, divide into bowls, sprinkle the parsley on top and serve as a party dip.

Nutritional Values per serving: Calories 170, fat 3, fiber 2, carbs 6, protein 7

Broccoli Spread

Preparation time: 10 minutes

Cooking time: 12 minutes

Servings: 4

Ingredients:

- 2 tablespoons avocado oil
- 8 garlic cloves, minced
- ½ cup veggie stock
- 6 cups broccoli florets
- A pinch of salt and black pepper
- 3 tablespoons cream cheese, soft

Directions:

1. Set your instant pot on Sauté mode, add the oil, heat it up, add the garlic and brown for 2 minutes.
2. Add the rest of the ingredients except the cream cheese, put the lid on and cook on Low for 10 minutes.
3. Release the pressure naturally for 10 minutes, transfer the broccoli mix to a blender, add the cream cheese, pulse well, divide into bowls and serve as a party spread.

Nutritional Values per serving: Calories 178, fat 3, fiber 3, carbs 5, protein 8

Cumin Cheese Spread

Preparation time: 5 minutes

Cooking time: 8 minutes

Servings: 4

Ingredients:

- 1 teaspoon olive oil
- 1 red onion, chopped
- 2 spring onions, chopped
- 1 cup cream cheese, soft
- 2 teaspoons cumin, ground
- ¼ teaspoon red pepper flakes
- A pinch of salt and black pepper
- 1 cup water

Directions:

1. In a bowl, combine the cream cheese with spring onions and the rest of the ingredients except the water, whisk really well and put everything in a ramekin.
2. Add the water to your instant pot, add the trivet and put the ramekin inside.
3. Put the lid on, cook on Low for 8 minutes, release the pressure fast for 5 minutes and serve the spread right away.

Nutritional Values per serving: Calories 170, fat 2, fiber 3, carbs 6, protein 8

Leeks and Bell Pepper Spread

Preparation time: 10 minutes

Cooking time: 15 minutes

Servings: 6

Ingredients:

- ¼ cup veggie stock
- 1 pound red bell peppers, chopped
- 4 leeks, sliced
- A pinch of salt and black pepper
- 1 tablespoon olive oil
- 1 tablespoon lemon juice
- 2 tablespoons cream cheese
- 2 garlic cloves, minced
- 1 tablespoon cilantro, chopped

Directions:

1. In your instant pot, combine the bell peppers with the leeks and the rest of the ingredients except the cream cheese and cilantro, put the lid on and cook on High for 15 minutes.
2. Release the pressure naturally for 10 minutes, transfer the mix to a blender, add the cream cheese and pulse well.
3. Divide into bowls and serve as a spread with the cilantro sprinkled on top.

Nutritional Values per serving: Calories 180, fat 4, fiber 3, carbs 7, protein 9

Chicken, Spinach and Avocado Salad

Preparation time: 10 minutes

Cooking time: 15 minutes

Servings: 4

Ingredients:

- 1 avocado, pitted, peeled and cubed
- 2 tablespoons Greek yogurt
- 2 tablespoons mayonnaise
- 2 spring onions, chopped
- 1 and ½ cups baby spinach
- 1 cup chicken stock
- A pinch of salt and black pepper
- 1 pound chicken breast, skinless, boneless and cubed

Directions:

1. In your instant pot, combine the chicken with salt, pepper and the stock, put the lid on and cook on High for 15 minutes.
2. Release the pressure naturally for 10 minutes, drain the chicken, transfer it to a bowl, add the rest of the ingredients, toss, divide into small bowls and serve as an appetizer.

Nutritional Values per serving: Calories 224, fat 12, fiber 4, carbs 7, protein 12

Pesto Barley Bowls

Preparation time: 5 minutes

Cooking time: 20 minutes

Servings: 4

Ingredients:

- 1 cup hulled barley, rinsed
- 2 cups veggie stock
- ¾ cup basil pesto
- 1 tablespoon chives, chopped
- 1 red onion, chopped
- 1 celery stalks chopped
- A pinch of salt and black pepper

Directions:

1. In your instant pot, combine the barley with the stock, salt and pepper, toss, put the lid on and cook on High for 20 minutes.
2. Release the pressure fast for 5 minutes, stir the barley, transfer to a bowl, add the rest of the ingredients and toss well.
3. Divide into cups and serve as an appetizer.

Nutritional Values per serving: Calories 172, fat 4, fiber 4, carbs 7, protein 9

Balsamic Olives Salsa

Preparation time: 5 minutes

Cooking time: 5 minutes

Servings: 4

Ingredients:

- 1 tablespoon balsamic vinegar
- 1 tablespoon olive oil
- 1 cup cherry tomatoes, halved
- 2 green onions, chopped
- 2 cups kalamata olives, pitted and chopped
- 1 handful basil leaves, chopped
- 1 handful parsley leaves, chopped

Directions:

1. Set your instant pot on Sauté mode, add the oil, heat it up, add the tomatoes and the rest of the ingredients, toss, put the lid on and cook on High for 5 minutes.
2. Release the pressure fast for 5 minutes, divide the salsa into bowls and serve cold as an appetizer.

Nutritional Values per serving: Calories 152, fat 2, fiber 3, carbs 6, protein 7

Cheese Dip with Peppers

Preparation Time: 10 minutes

Servings 8

Nutritional Values per serving: 237 Calories; 20.6g Fat; 3.1g Total Carbs; 10.2g Protein; 1.8g Sugars

Ingredients

- 1 tablespoon butter
- 2 red bell peppers, sliced
- 1 teaspoon red Aleppo pepper flakes
- 1 cup cream cheese, room temperature
- 2 cups Colby cheese, shredded
- 1 teaspoon sumac
- 2 garlic cloves, minced
- 1 cup chicken broth
- Salt and ground black pepper, to taste

Directions

1. Press the "Sauté" button to heat up your Instant Pot. Once hot, melt the butter. Sauté the peppers until just tender.
2. Add the remaining ingredients; gently stir to combine.
3. Secure the lid. Choose "Manual" mode and High pressure; cook for 3 minutes. Once cooking is complete, use a quick pressure release; carefully remove the lid.
4. Serve with your favorite keto dippers. Bon appétit!

Juicy Chicken Drumettes

Preparation Time: 15 minutes

Servings 8

Nutritional Values per serving: 237 Calories; 20.6g Fat; 3.1g Total Carbs; 10.2g Protein; 1.8g Sugars

Ingredients

- 2 pounds chicken drumettes
- 1 stick butter
- 1 tablespoon coconut aminos
- Sea salt and ground black pepper, to taste
- 1/2 teaspoon dried dill weed
- 1/2 teaspoon dried basil
- 1 teaspoon hot sauce
- 1 tablespoon fish sauce
- 1/2 cup tomato sauce
- 1/2 cup water

Directions

1. Add all ingredients to your Instant Pot.
2. Secure the lid. Choose "Poultry" mode and High pressure; cook for 10 minutes. Once cooking is complete, use a natural pressure release; carefully remove the lid.
3. Serve at room temperature and enjoy!

Creamy Cauliflower Bites

Preparation Time: 25 minutes

Servings 8

Nutritional Values per serving: 157 Calories; 12.1g Fat; 3.6g Total Carbs; 8.9g Protein; 1.2g Sugars

Ingredients

- 1 head of cauliflower, broken into florets
- 2 tablespoons butter
- Coarse sea salt and white pepper, to taste
- 1/2 teaspoon cayenne pepper
- 1 garlic clove, minced
- 1/2 cup Parmesan cheese, grated
- 1 cup Asiago cheese, shredded
- 2 tablespoons fresh chopped chives, minced
- 2 eggs, beaten

Directions

1. Add 1 cup of water and a steamer basket to the Instant Pot. Now, add cauliflower to the steamer basket.
2. Secure the lid. Choose "Manual" mode and High pressure; cook for 3 minutes. Once cooking is complete, use a quick pressure release; carefully remove the lid.
3. Transfer the cauliflower to a food processor. Add the remaining ingredients; process until everything is well incorporated.
4. Shape the mixture into balls. Bake in the preheated oven at 400 degrees F for 18 minutes. Bon appétit!

Yummy Baby Carrots

Preparation Time: 10 minutes

Servings 8

Nutritional Values per serving: 94 Calories; 6.1g Fat; 5.9g Total Carbs; 1.4g Protein; 3.1g Sugars

Ingredients

- 28 ounces baby carrots
- 1 cup chicken broth
- 1/2 cup water
- 1/2 stick butter
- 2 tablespoons balsamic vinegar
- Coarse sea salt, to taste
- 1/2 teaspoon red pepper flakes, crushed
- 1/2 teaspoon dried dill weed

Directions

1. Simply add all of the above ingredients to your Instant Pot.
2. Secure the lid. Choose "Manual" mode and High pressure; cook for 3 minutes. Once cooking is complete, use a quick pressure release; carefully remove the lid.
3. Transfer to a nice serving bowl and serve. Enjoy!

Cheesy Keto Dip

Preparation Time: 10 minutes

Servings 10

Nutritional Values per serving: 280 Calories; 20.4g Fat; 3.7g Total Carbs; 20.6g Protein; 2.5g Sugars

Ingredients

- 10 ounces cream cheese
- 10 ounces Pepper-Jack cheese
- 1 pound tomatoes, pureed
- 10 ounces pancetta, chopped
- 1 cup green olives, pitted and halved
- 1/2 teaspoon garlic powder
- 1 teaspoon dried oregano
- 1 cup chicken broth
- 4 ounces Mozzarella cheese, thinly sliced

Directions

1. Combine cream cheese, Pepper-Jack cheese, tomatoes, pancetta, olives, garlic, powder, and oregano in your Instant Pot.
2. Secure the lid. Choose "Manual" mode and High pressure; cook for 4 minutes. Once cooking is complete, use a quick pressure release; carefully remove the lid.
3. Top with Mozzarella cheese; cover and let it sit in the residual heat. Serve warm or at room temperature. Bon appétit!

Simple Brussels Sprouts

Preparation Time: 10 minutes

Servings 4

Nutritional Values per serving: 68 Calories; 3.3g Fat; 5.8g Total Carbs; 3.5g Protein; 1.9g Sugars

Ingredients

- 1 tablespoon butter
- 1/2 cup shallots, chopped
- 3/4 pound whole Brussels sprouts
- Sea salt, to taste
- 1/4 teaspoon ground black pepper
- 1/2 cup water
- 1/2 cup chicken stock

Directions

1. Press the "Sauté" button to heat up your Instant Pot. Once hot, melt the butter and sauté the shallots until tender and translucent.
2. Add the remaining ingredients to the Instant Pot.
3. Secure the lid. Choose "Manual" mode and High pressure; cook for 4 minutes. Once cooking is complete, use a quick pressure release; carefully remove the lid.
4. Transfer Brussels sprouts to a serving platter. Serve with cocktail sticks and enjoy!

Quick Spinach Dip

Preparation Time: 5 minutes

Servings 10

Nutritional Values per serving: 43 Calories; 1.7g Fat; 3.5g Total Carbs; 4.1g Protein; 1.3g Sugars

Ingredients

- 1 pound spinach
- 4 ounces Cottage cheese, at room temperature
- 4 ounces Cheddar cheese, grated
- 1 teaspoon garlic powder
- 1/2 teaspoon shallot powder
- 1/2 teaspoon celery seeds
- 1/2 teaspoon fennel seeds
- 1/2 teaspoon cayenne pepper
- Salt and black pepper, to taste

Directions

1. Add all of the above ingredients to your Instant Pot.
2. Serve warm or at room temperature. Bon appétit!
3. Secure the lid. Choose "Manual" mode and High pressure; cook for 1 minute. Once cooking is complete, use a quick pressure release; carefully remove the lid.

Asparagus with Mayo Dip

Preparation Time: 5 minutes

Servings 6

Nutritional Values per serving: 116 Calories; 8.5g Fat; 6.9g Total Carbs; 4.5g Protein; 2.4g Sugars

Ingredients

- 1 ½ pounds asparagus spears, trimmed
- 1/2 cup sour cream
- 1/2 cup mayonnaise
- 2 tablespoons fresh chervil
- 2 tablespoons scallions, chopped
- 1 teaspoon garlic, minced
- Salt, to taste

Directions

- Add 1 cup of water and a steamer basket to you Instant Pot.
- Secure the lid. Choose "Manual" mode and High pressure; cook for 1 minute. Once cooking is complete, use a quick pressure release; carefully remove the lid.
- Then, thoroughly combine the remaining ingredients to make your dipping sauce. Serve your asparagus with the dipping sauce on the side. Bon appétit!

Keto Greens Dip

Preparation Time: 10 minutes

Servings 10

Nutritional Values per serving: 153 Calories; 10.6g Fat; 5g Total Carbs; 8.7g Protein; 3.1g Sugars

Ingredients

- 2 tablespoons butter, melted
- 20 ounces mustard greens
- 2 bell peppers, chopped
- 1 white onion, chopped
- 1 teaspoon garlic, minced
- Sea salt and ground black pepper, to taste
- 1 cup chicken stock
- 8 ounces Neufchâtel cheese, crumbled
- 1/2 teaspoon dried thyme
- 1/2 teaspoon dried dill
- 1/2 teaspoon turmeric powder
- 3/4 cup Romano cheese, preferably freshly grated

Directions

1. Add the butter, mustard greens, bell peppers, onion, and garlic to the Instant Pot.
2. Secure the lid. Choose "Manual" mode and High pressure; cook for 3 minutes. Once cooking is complete, use a quick pressure release; carefully remove the lid.
3. Then, add the remaining ingredients and press the "Sauté" button. Let it simmer until the cheese is melted; then, gently stir this mixture until everything is well incorporated.
4. Serve with your favorite low-carb dippers.

Cocktail Sausages Asian-Style

Preparation Time: 10 minutes

Servings 8

Nutritional Values per serving: 330 Calories; 24.8g Fat; 2.7g Total Carbs; 22.7g Protein; 1.2g Sugars

Ingredients

- 1 teaspoon sesame oil
- 20 mini cocktail sausages
- 1/2 cup tomato puree
- 1/2 cup chicken stock
- 1 tablespoon dark soy sauce
- 1/3 teaspoon ground black pepper
- 1/2 teaspoon paprika
- Himalayan salt, to taste
- 1/2 teaspoon mustard seeds
- 1/2 teaspoon fennel seeds
- 1/4 teaspoon fresh ginger root, peeled and grated
- 1 teaspoon garlic paste

Directions

1. Simply throw all ingredients into your Instant Pot.
2. Secure the lid. Choose "Manual" mode and High pressure; cook for 4 minutes. Once cooking is complete, use a quick pressure release; carefully remove the lid.
3. Serve with cocktail sticks and enjoy!

Stuffed Mushrooms with Cheese

Preparation Time: 10 minutes

Servings 5

Nutritional Values per serving: 151 Calories; 9.2g Fat; 6g Total Carbs; 11.9g Protein; 3.6g Sugars

Ingredients

- 1 tablespoon butter, softened
- 1 shallot, chopped
- 2 cloves garlic, minced
- 1 ½ cups Cottage cheese, at room temperature
- 1/2 cup Romano cheese, grated
- 1 red bell pepper, chopped
- 1 green bell pepper, chopped
- 1 jalapeno pepper, minced
- 1/2 teaspoon dried basil
- 1/2 teaspoon dried oregano
- 1/2 teaspoon dried rosemary
- 10 medium-sized button mushrooms, stems removed

Directions

1. Press the "Sauté" button to heat up your Instant Pot. Once hot, melt the butter and sauté the shallots until tender and translucent.
2. Stir in the garlic and cook an additional 30 seconds or until aromatic. Now, add the remaining ingredients, except for the mushroom caps, and stir to combine well.
3. Then, fill the mushroom caps with this mixture.
4. Add 1 cup of water and a steamer basket to you Instant Pot. Arrange the stuffed mushrooms in the steamer basket.
5. Secure the lid. Choose "Manual" mode and High pressure; cook for 5 minutes. Once cooking is complete, use a quick pressure release; carefully remove the lid.
6. Arrange the stuffed mushroom on a serving platter and serve. Enjoy!

Family Meatballs

Preparation Time: 15 minutes

Servings 6

Nutritional Values per serving: 384 Calories; 22.2g Fat; 6.1g Total Carbs; 38.4g Protein; 3.6g Sugars

Ingredients

- 1/2 pound ground pork
- 1 pound ground beef
- 1/2 cup Romano cheese, grated
- 1/2 cup pork rinds, crushed
- 1 egg, beaten
- Coarse sea salt and ground black pepper, to taste
- 1 teaspoon granulated garlic
- 1/2 teaspoon cayenne pepper
- 1/2 teaspoon dried basil
- 1/4 cup milk, lukewarm
- 1 ½ cups BBQ sauce

Directions

1. Thoroughly combine ground meat, cheese, pork rinds, egg, salt, black pepper, garlic, cayenne pepper, basil, and milk in the mixing bowl.
2. Then, roll the mixture into 20 meatballs.
3. Pour BBQ sauce into your Instant Pot. Now, add the meatballs and secure the lid.
4. Choose "Manual" mode and High pressure; cook for 8 minutes. Once cooking is complete, use a quick pressure release; carefully remove the lid. Bon appétit!

Fresh Keto Meatballs

Preparation Time: 15 minutes

Servings 6

Nutritional Values per serving: 280 Calories; 20.4g Fat; 3.7g Total Carbs; 20.6g Protein; 2.5g Sugars

Ingredients

- 1/2 pound ground pork
- 1/2 pound ground turkey
- 2 eggs
- 1/3 cup almond flour
- Sea salt and ground black pepper, to taste
- 2 garlic cloves, minced
- 1 cup Romano cheese, grated
- 1 teaspoon dried basil
- 1/2 teaspoon dried thyme
- 1/4 cup minced fresh mint, plus more for garnish
- 1/2 cup beef bone broth
- 1/2 cup tomatoes, puréed
- 2 tablespoons scallions

Directions

1. Thoroughly combine all ingredients, except for broth, tomatoes, and scallions in a mixing bowl.
2. Shape the mixture into 2-inch meatballs and reserve.
3. Add beef bone broth, tomatoes, and scallions to your Instant Pot. Place the meatballs in this sauce.
4. Secure the lid. Choose "Manual" mode and High pressure; cook for 8 minutes. Once cooking is complete, use a quick pressure release; carefully remove the lid. Bon appétit!
5. Parmigiano Chicken Wings

Preparation Time: 20 minutes

Servings 12

Nutritional Values per serving: 443 Calories; 30.8g Fat; 6.2g Total Carbs; 33.2g Protein; 3.5g Sugars

Ingredients

- 4 pounds chicken wings cut into sections
- 1/2 cup butter, melted
- 1 tablespoon Italian seasoning mix
- 1/2 teaspoon onion powder
- 1/2 teaspoon garlic powder
- 1 teaspoon paprika
- 1/2 teaspoon coarse sea salt
- 1/2 teaspoon ground black pepper
- 1 cup Parmigiano-Reggiano cheese, shaved
- 2 eggs, lightly whisked

Directions

1. Add chicken wings, butter, Italian seasoning mix, onion powder, garlic powder, paprika, salt, and black pepper to your Instant Pot.
2. Secure the lid. Choose "Poultry" mode and High pressure. Cook the chicken wings for 10 minutes. Once cooking is complete, use a natural pressure release; carefully remove the lid.
3. Mix Parmigiano-Reggiano cheese with eggs. Spoon this mixture over the wings.
4. Secure the lid. Choose "Manual" mode and High pressure; cook for 4 minutes longer. Once cooking is complete, use a quick pressure release; carefully remove the lid. Bon appétit!

Delicious Cauliflower Tots

Preparation Time: 25 minutes

Servings 6

Nutritional Values per serving: 132 Calories; 8.7g Fat; 4.5g Total Carbs; 9.2g Protein; 1.3g Sugars

Ingredients

- 1 head of cauliflower, broken into florets
- 2 eggs, beaten
- 1 shallot, peeled and chopped
- 1/2 cup Swiss cheese, grated
- 1/2 cup Parmesan cheese, grated
- 2 tablespoons fresh coriander, chopped
- Sea salt and ground black pepper, to taste

Directions

1. Start by adding 1 cup of water and a steamer basket to your Instant Pot.
2. Arrange the cauliflower florets in the steamer basket.
3. Secure the lid. Choose "Manual" mode and High pressure; cook for 3 minutes. Once cooking is complete, use a quick pressure release; carefully remove the lid.
4. Mash the cauliflower and add the remaining ingredients. Form the mixture into a tater-tot shape with oiled hands.
5. Place cauliflower tots on a lightly greased baking sheet. Bake in the preheated oven at 390 degrees F approximately 20 minutes; make sure to flip them halfway through the cooking time.
6. Serve at room temperature. Bon appétit!

Keto Broccoli Balls

Preparation Time: 25 minutes

Servings 8

Nutritional Values per serving: 137 Calories; 9.5g Fat; 4.8g Total Carbs; 8.9g Protein; 1.5g Sugars

Ingredients

- 1 head broccoli, broken into florets
- 1/2 cup Añejo cheese, shredded
- 1 ½ cups Cotija cheese, crumbled
- 3 ounces Ricotta cheese, cut into small chunks
- 1 teaspoon chili pepper flakes

Directions

1. Add 1 cup of water and a steamer basket to the Instant Pot.
2. Place broccoli florets in the steamer basket.
3. Secure the lid. Choose "Manual" mode and Low pressure; cook for 5 minutes. Once cooking is complete, use a quick pressure release; carefully remove the lid.
4. Add the broccoli florets along with the remaining ingredients to your food processor. Process until everything is well incorporated.
5. Shape the mixture into balls and place your balls on a parchment-lined baking sheet. Bake in the preheated oven at 390 degrees F for 15 minutes. Bon appétit!

Cheesy Taco Dip

Preparation Time: 10 minutes

Servings 12

Nutritional Values per serving: 275 Calories; 23.7g Fat; 2.6g Total Carbs; 12.4g Protein; 1.2g Sugars

Ingredients

- 2 teaspoons sesame oil
- 1/2 cup yellow onion, chopped
- 1 pound ground turkey
- 1 teaspoon roasted garlic paste
- 1 teaspoon ancho chili powder
- 1/2 teaspoon dried basil
- 1/2 teaspoon dried Mexican oregano
- 1/4 teaspoon freshly ground black pepper, or more to taste
- Sea salt, to taste
- 10 ounces Ricotta cheese, at room temperature
- 1 cup Mexican cheese, shredded
- 1 cup broth, preferably homemade
- 2 ripe tomatoes, chopped
- 1/3 cup salsa verde

Directions

1. Press the "Sauté" button to heat up your Instant Pot. Once hot, heat the sesame oil; now, sauté the onion until translucent.
2. Stir in ground turkey and continue to sauté until it is no longer pink. Add the remaining ingredients and stir until everything is combined well.
3. Secure the lid. Choose "Manual" mode and High pressure; cook for 6 minutes. Once cooking is complete, use a natural pressure release; carefully remove the lid. Bon appétit!

Meatballs with Cheese

Preparation Time: 15 minutes

Servings 8

Nutritional Values per serving: 277 Calories; 17.4g Fat; 3.1g Total Carbs; 25.8g Protein; 0.9g Sugars

Ingredients

- 1 pound ground beef
- 1/2 cup pork chicharron, crushed
- 1/2 cup Parmesan cheese, grated
- 2 eggs, beaten
- 2 tablespoons fresh scallions, chopped
- 2 tablespoons fresh cilantro, chopped
- 1 teaspoon garlic, minced
- Sea salt, to your liking
- 1/2 teaspoon ground black pepper
- 1/2 teaspoon cayenne pepper
- 1 cup Colby cheese, cubed
- 2 teaspoons olive oil
- 1/2 cup chicken broth
- 1/2 cup BBQ sauce

Directions

1. In a mixing dish, thoroughly combine ground beef, pork chicharron, Parmesan cheese, eggs, scallions, cilantro, garlic, salt, black pepper, and cayenne pepper; mix until everything is well incorporated.
2. Now, shape the mixture into balls. Press one cheese cube into center of each meatball, sealing it inside.
3. Press the "Sauté" button and heat the olive oil. Sear the meatballs for a couple of minutes or until browned on all sides. Pour in chicken broth and BBQ sauce.
4. Secure the lid. Choose the "Manual" setting and cook for 8 minutes under High pressure. Once cooking is complete, use a quick pressure release; carefully remove the lid.
5. Serve your meatballs with the sauce. Bon appétit!

Spanish Fat Bombs

Preparation Time: 10 minutes

Servings 8

Nutritional Values per serving: 307 Calories; 26.8g Fat; 5.1g Total Carbs; 10.9g Protein; 2.9g Sugars

Ingredients

- 1 tablespoon tallow, melted
- 1 yellow onion, chopped
- 1 pound Chorizo sausage
- 1 garlic clove, minced
- 1 red bell pepper, chopped
- 1 cup chicken broth
- 1/2 teaspoon deli mustard
- 1 plum tomato, puréed
- 10 ounces Halloumi cheese, crumbled
- 1/3 cup mayonnaise

Directions

1. Press the "Sauté" button and melt the tallow. Once hot, cook the onion until tender and translucent.
2. Add Chorizo and garlic to your Instant Pot; cook until the sausage is no longer pink; crumble the sausage with a fork.
3. Now, stir in bell pepper, broth, mustard, and tomato.
4. Secure the lid. Choose "Manual" mode and High pressure; cook for 4 minutes. Once cooking is complete, use a quick pressure release; carefully remove the lid.
5. Add the cheese and mayo. Shape the mixture into 2-inch balls and serve. Bon appétit!

Yummy Cocktail Wieners

Preparation Time: 10 minutes

Servings 10

Nutritional Values per serving: 257 Calories; 22.7g Fat; 1.4g Total Carbs; 10.8g Protein; 0.2g Sugars

Ingredients

- 1 pound cocktail wieners
- 1/2 pound sliced bacon, cold cut into slices
- 1/2 cup chicken broth
- 1/2 cup water
- 1/4 cup low-carb ketchup
- 2 tablespoons apple cider vinegar
- 1 tablespoon onion powder
- 1 tablespoon ground mustard
- Salt and pepper to taste

Directions

1. Wrap each cocktail wiener with a slice of bacon; secure with a toothpick.
2. Then, place one layer of bacon wrapped cocktail wieners in the bottom of the Instant Pot. Repeat layering until you run out of the cocktail wieners.
3. In a mixing bowl, thoroughly combine the remaining ingredients. Pour this mixture over the bacon wrapped cocktail wieners.
4. Secure the lid. Choose "Manual" mode and Low pressure; cook for 3 minutes. Once cooking is complete, use a natural pressure release; carefully remove the lid. Enjoy!

Fresh Brussels Sprouts with Aioli Sauce

Preparation Time: 10 minutes

Servings 4

Nutritional Values per serving: 161 Calories; 13.4g Fat; 6g Total Carbs; 3.1g Protein; 2.5g Sugars

Ingredients

- 1 tablespoon butter
- 1/2 cup scallions, chopped
- 3/4 pound Brussels sprouts
- Aioli Sauce:
- 1/4 cup mayonnaise
- 1 garlic clove, minced
- 1 tablespoon fresh lemon juice
- 1/2 teaspoon Dijon mustard

Directions

1. Press the "Sauté" button and melt the butter. Once hot, cook the scallions until softened. Now, add Brussels sprouts and sauté them for 1 minute more.
2. Secure the lid. Choose "Manual" mode and High pressure; cook for 4 minutes. Once cooking is complete, use a quick pressure release; carefully remove the lid.
3. Meanwhile, mix mayonnaise, garlic, lemon juice, Dijon mustard. Serve Brussels sprouts with Aioli sauce on the side. Bon appétit!

Cheesy Bacon Bites

Preparation Time: 10 minutes

Servings 8

Nutritional Values per serving: 187 Calories; 14.2g Fat; 5.2g Total Carbs; 9.4g Protein; 3.4g Sugars

Ingredients

- 1/2 pound rutabaga, grated
- 4 slices meaty bacon, chopped
- 7 ounces Gruyère cheese, shredded
- 3 eggs, beaten
- 3 tablespoons almond flour
- 1 teaspoon granulated garlic
- 1 teaspoon shallot powder
- Sea salt and ground black pepper, to taste

Directions

1. Add 1 cup of water and a metal trivet to the Instant Pot.
2. Mix all of the above ingredients until everything is well incorporated.
3. Put the mixture into a silicone pod tray that is previously greased with a nonstick cooking spray. Cover the tray with a sheet of aluminum foil and lower it onto the trivet.
4. Secure the lid. Choose "Manual" mode and Low pressure; cook for 5 minutes. Once cooking is complete, use a quick pressure release; carefully remove the lid. Bon appétit!

Juicy Meatballs

Preparation Time: 25 MIN

Serving: 8

Ingredients:

- 1 pound grass-fed ground chicken
- 1 organic egg
- 1/3 cup almond flour
- ½ tsp garlic powder
- Salt and freshly ground black pepper, to taste
- ¾ cup hot sauce
- 2 tbsp. olive oil
- 2 tbsp. melted butter
- ½ cup blue cheese dressing

Directions:

1. In a bowl, add all ingredients except, oil, hot sauce, butter and blue cheese dressing and mix until well combined.
2. Make equal sized meatballs from the mixture.
3. Place the oil in the Instant Pot and select "Sauté". Then add the meatballs and cook for about 4-5 minutes or until browned from all sides.

4. Meanwhile, in a bowl, mix together hot sauce and butter.
5. Select the "Cancel" and place butter mixture over meatballs.
6. Secure the lid and place the pressure valve to "Seal" position.
7. Select the "Poultry" and just use the default time of 5 minutes.
8. Select the "Cancel" and carefully do a Quick release.
9. Remove the lid and serve immediately with the topping of dressing.

Nutritional Values per serving:

Calories 278

Total Fat 21.6g

Net Carbs 0.33g

Protein 19g

Fiber 0.6g

Perfect Chicken Wings

Preparation Time: 40 MIN

Serving: 4

Ingredients:

- 1½ pounds grass-fed chicken wings
- ¼ cup sugar-free tomato puree
- 2-3 drops liquid stevia
- 1 tbsp. fresh lemon juice
- Salt and freshly ground black pepper, to taste

Directions:

1. In the bottom of Instant Pot, arrange a steamer trivet and pour 1 cup of water.
2. Place the pan on top of the trivet.
3. Place chicken wings on top of the trivet, standing vertically.
4. Secure the lid and place the pressure valve to "Seal" position.
5. Select "Manual" and cook under "High Pressure" for about 10 minutes.
6. Preheat the oven to broiler.
7. Select the "Cancel" and carefully do a Quick release.
8. Meanwhile, in a bowl, add remaining ingredients and beat until well combined.

9. Remove the lid and transfer chicken wings to the bowl of sauce.
10. Coat the wings with sauce generously.
11. Arrange the chicken wings onto a parchment paper lined baking sheet and broil for about 5 minutes.
12. Serve hot with remaining sauce.

Nutritional Values per serving:

Calories 330

Total Fat 12.7g

Net Carbs 0.37g

Protein 49.5g

Fiber 0.3g

2-Ingredients Chicken Wings

Preparation Time: 40 MIN

Serving: 6

Ingredients:

- 2 pounds grass-fed chicken wings and drumettes
- ½ cup sugar-free BBQ sauce

Directions:

1. In the bottom of Instant Pot, arrange a steamer basket and pour 1 cup of water.
2. Place the wings and drumettes into the steamer basket.
3. Secure the lid and place the pressure valve to "Seal" position.
4. Select "Manual" and cook under "High Pressure" for about 5 minutes.
5. Preheat the oven to 450 degrees F. Arrange a wire rack on a baking sheet.
6. Select the "Cancel" and carefully do a Natural release.
7. Remove the lid and transfer wings and drumettes to a large plate.
8. With paper towels, pat dry the wings and drumettes.
9. In a bowl, add wings and drumettes with BBQ sauce and toss to coat well.

10. Place the wings and drumettes onto the prepared baking sheet in a single layer.
11. Bake for about 8-15 minutes.
12. Remove from oven and serve warm.

Nutritional Values per serving:

Calories 319

Total Fat 11.3g

Net Carbs 1.26g

Protein 43.7g

Fiber 0.1g

Sticky Chicken Wings

Preparation Time: 40 MIN

Serving: 8

Ingredients:

- 3 pounds drum and wings separated grass-fed chicken wings
- 6 tbsp. olive oil (divided
- 1 cup sugar-free teriyaki sauce
- 1 tbsp. fresh lemon juice
- 1 tbsp. Erythritol
- ½ tsp crushed red pepper flakes

Directions:

1. In a large bowl, add chicken wings, 4 tablespoons of oil, teriyaki sauce, lemon juice and Erythritol and mix well.
2. Refrigerate for at least 2 hours.
3. Remove chicken wings from the bowl, reserving marinade.
4. Place the remaining oil in the Instant Pot and select "Sauté". Then add the wings and cook for about -4 minutes or until browned from all sides.
5. Select the "Cancel" and place reserved marinade over wings evenly.

6. Secure the lid and place the pressure valve to "Seal" position.
7. Select "Manual" and cook under "High Pressure" for about 7 minutes.
8. Preheat the oven to broiler.
9. Select the "Cancel" and carefully do a "Natural" release for about 10 minutes and then do a "Quick" release.
10. Remove the lid and transfer the wings onto a baking sheet in a single layer.
11. Broil for about 6-8 minutes.
12. Remove from oven and serve warm with the sprinkling of red pepper flakes.

Nutritional Values per serving:

Calories 446

Total Fat 23.2g

Net Carbs 0.95g

Protein 51.4g

Fiber 0.1g

Simple Boiled Peanuts

Preparation Time: 1½ HOUR

Serving: 6

Ingredients:

1 pound raw peanuts in the shell

1/3 cup coarse sea salt

Filtered water, as required

Directions:

1. Rinse the peanuts under cold running water and remove any twigs and roots.
2. In the bottom of Instant Pot, place peanuts, salt and enough water to cover the peanuts and stir.
3. Place a plate or trivet on top of peanuts.
4. Secure the lid and place the pressure valve to "Seal" position.
5. Select "Manual" and cook under "High Pressure" for about 80 minutes.
6. Select the "Cancel" and carefully do a "Natural" release.
7. Remove the lid and keep aside to cool.
8. Drain well and serve.

Nutritional Values per serving:

Calories 429

Total Fat 37.2g

Net Carbs 2.03g

Protein 19.5g

Fiber 6.4g

Southern Boiled Peanuts

Preparation Time: 1 HOUR 40 MIN

Serving: 6

Ingredients:

- 1 pound jumbo raw peanuts
- ½ cup sea salt
- 1 tbsp. Cajun seasoning
- Filtered water, as required

Directions:

1. Rinse the peanuts under cold running water and remove any twigs and roots.
2. In the bottom of Instant Pot, place peanuts, salt, Cajun seasoning and enough water to cover the peanuts and stir.
3. Place a plate or trivet on top of peanuts.
4. Secure the lid and place the pressure valve to "Seal" position.
5. Select "Manual" and cook under "High Pressure" for about 65-90 minutes.
6. Select the "Cancel" and carefully do a "Natural" release.
7. Remove the lid and keep aside to cool.
8. Drain well and serve.

Nutritional Values per serving:

Calories 429

Total Fat 37.2g

Net Carbs 2.03g

Protein 19.5g

Fiber 6.4g

Hard Boiled Eggs

Preparation Time: 10 MIN

Serving: 4

Ingredients:

- 8 large Eggs
- 1 cup Water

Instructions:

1. Set the wire rack in the Instant Pot and pour in the water.
2. Carefully place eggs in and place and lock the lid.
3. Manually set the cooking time to 4 minutes at high pressure.
4. Quick release the pressure and transfer the eggs in iced water for 5 minutes for easier peeling.
5. Use immediately or store in the fridge for later use.

Nutritional Values per serving:

Calories: 156

Total Fats: 10.6g

Net Carbs: 1.1g

Proteins: 12.6g

Fibers: 0g

Steamed Artichokes

Preparation Time: 20 MIN

Serving: 4

Ingredients:

- 4 medium Artichokes
- 1 wedge Lemon
- 1 cup Water

Directions:

1. Wash the artichokes well and with a knife cut off the stem and around an inch of the top.
2. Rub the cut on top with the lemon, to prevent browning, and gently spread the leaves a bit.
3. Place the artichokes in a steamer insert in the Instant Pot and pour in a cup of water.
4. Place and lock the lid, and set the Instant Pot manual to 10 minutes cooking time at high pressure.
5. When done let the Instant Pot naturally release the pressure for 10 minutes and then open the valve for quick release.
6. Serve warm with a dipping sauce.

Nutritional Values per serving:

Calories: 60

Total Fats: 0.2g

Net Carbs: 6.6g

Proteins: 4.2g

Fibers: 6.9g

Zingy Boiled Peanuts

Preparation Time: 1 HOUR 40 MIN

Serving: 6

Ingredients:

- 1 pound raw peanuts
- 1/3 cup Old Bay seasoning
- ¼ cup kosher salt
- ¼ cup apple cider vinegar
- 1 tbsp. mustard seeds
- 1 bay leaf
- Filtered water, as required

Directions:

1. Rinse the peanuts under cold running water and remove any twigs and roots.
2. In the bottom of Instant Pot, add all ingredients and enough water to cover the peanuts and stir.
3. Place a plate or trivet on top of peanuts.
4. Secure the lid and place the pressure valve to "Seal" position.
5. Select "Manual" and cook under "High Pressure" for about 75-90 minutes.
6. Select the "Cancel" and carefully do a "Natural" release.
7. Remove the lid and keep aside to cool.

8. Drain well and serve.

Nutritional Values per serving:

Calories 4540

Total Fat 37.8g

Net Carbs 0.48g

Protein 20g

Fiber 6.7g

Unique Party Food

Preparation Time: 18 MIN

Serving: 4

Ingredients:

- 1 pound asparagus spears
- 8-ounce sliced prosciutto

Directions:

1. Wrap the prosciutto slices around asparagus spears.
2. In the bottom of Instant Pot, arrange a steamer basket and pour 2 cups of water.
3. Place the carrots into the steamer basket.
4. Arrange any extra un-wrapped spears in the bottom of the steamer basket in a single layer.
5. Place prosciutto-wrapped asparagus on top in a single layer.
6. Secure the lid and place the pressure valve to "Seal" position.
7. Select "Manual" and cook under "High Pressure" for about 2-3 minutes.
8. Select the "Cancel" and carefully do a Natural release.
9. Remove the lid and serve warm

Nutritional Values per serving:

Calories 105

Total Fat 3.3g

Net Carbs 1.32 g

Protein 14.4g

Fiber 2,1g

Decadent Liver Pâté

Preparation Time: 25 MIN

Serving: 6

Ingredients:

- 1 tsp olive oil
- 1 roughly chopped medium yellow onion
- Salt and freshly ground black pepper, to taste
- ¾ pound grass-fed chicken livers
- 1 bay leaf
- ¼ cup homemade chicken broth
- 1 tbsp. fresh lemon juice
- 2 anchovies in oil
- 1 tbsp. capers
- 1 tbsp. butter

Directions:

1. Place the oil in the Instant Pot and select "Sauté". Then add the onion with a little salt and black pepper and cook for about 2-3 minutes.
2. Add the chicken livers and bay leaf and cook for about 2 minutes.
3. Add the broth and scrape brown bits from the bottom.
4. Select the "Cancel" and stir the mixture once.

5. Secure the lid and place the pressure valve to "Seal" position.
6. Select "Manual" and cook under "High Pressure" for about 5 minutes.
7. Select the "Cancel" and carefully do a Natural release.
8. Remove the lid and discard the bay leaf.
9. Stir in anchovies and capers and with a stick blender, blend the mixture until pureed.
10. Stir in butter and rum and transfer to a bowl.
11. Refrigerate to chill before serving.

Nutritional Values per serving:

Calories 142

Total Fat 7.3g

Net Carbs 0.4g

Protein 15.7g

Fiber 0.5g

Exotic Mushroom Pâté

Preparation Time: 25 MIN

Serving: 6

Ingredients:

- 1 cup boiling water
- ¾ cup rinsed dry porcini mushrooms
- 2 tbsp. unsalted butter
- 1 sliced small yellow onion
- 1 pound thinly sliced fresh cremini mushrooms
- 2-3 tbsp. homemade chicken broth
- 1 tbsp. fresh lemon juice
- 1 bay leaf
- Salt and ground white pepper, to taste
- 1 tbsp. extra-virgin olive oil
- 3 tbsp. finely grated Parmigiana Reggiano cheese

Directions:

1. In a heat-proof bowl, mix together boiling water and dry porcini mushrooms.
2. Cover the bowl tightly and keep aside.
3. Place the butter in the Instant Pot and select "Sauté". Then add the onion and cook for about 5 minutes.
4. Add the fresh mushrooms and cook for about 5 minutes.

5. Add broth and lemon juice and cook for about 5 minutes or until all the liquid is absorbed.
6. Select the "Cancel" and stir in porcini mushrooms and with soaking liquid, bay leaf, salt and black pepper.
7. Secure the lid and place the pressure valve to "Seal" position.
8. Select "Manual" and cook under "High Pressure" for about 12 minutes.
9. Select the "Cancel" and carefully do a Natural release.
10. Remove the lid and discard the bay leaf.
11. Add the olive oil and with an immersion blender, blend the mixture until smooth.
12. Add the cheese and blend until well combined.
13. Transfer the mixture to a bowl and refrigerate for about 2 hours before serving.

Nutritional Values per serving:

Calories 115

Total Fat 6.6g

Net Carbs 0.96g

Protein 6.3g

Fiber 0.7g

Garden Fresh Salsa

Preparation Time: 30 MIN

Serving: 20

Ingredients:

- 4 cups cored, peeled and chopped tomatoes
- 1 (15-ouncecan sugar-free tomato sauce
- 1 (6-ouncecan sugar-free tomato paste
- 1 chopped medium yellow onion
- 2 seeded and chopped large green bell peppers
- 3 seeded and chopped jalapeño peppers
- 4 minced garlic cloves
- ½ cup apple cider vinegar
- 1 tbsp. hot sauce
- 1 tbsp. ground cumin
- Kosher salt, to taste

Directions:

1. In the bottom of Instant Pot, place all ingredients and stir to combine.
2. Secure the lid and place the pressure valve to "Seal" position.
3. Select "Manual" and cook under "High Pressure" for about 15 minutes.
4. Select the "Cancel" and carefully do a "Natural" release.

5. Remove the lid and keep aside to cool for about 20 minutes.
6. Transfer the salsa into wide mouth pint jars and seal with lids.
7. Refrigerate to chill before serving.

Nutritional Values per serving:

Calories 29

Total Fat 0.3g

Net Carbs 0.30g

Protein 1.3g

Fiber 1.5g

Party Meatballs

Preparation Time: 40 MIN

Serving: 8

Ingredients:

- 1 pound lean ground turkey
- 1 organic egg
- ¼ tsp dried thyme
- ¼ tsp dried oregano
- ¼ tsp dried rosemary
- ¼ tsp garlic powder
- Salt and freshly ground black pepper, to taste
- 1½ cups sugar-free tomato sauce

Directions:

1. In a bowl, add all ingredients except tomato sauce and mix until well combined.
2. Make equal sized meatballs from the mixture.
3. In the bottom of Instant Pot, place meatballs and tomato sauce and gently stir to combine.
4. Secure the lid and place the pressure valve to "Seal" position.
5. Select "Manual" and cook under "High Pressure" for about 25 minutes.
6. Select the "Cancel" and carefully do a "Quick" release.

7. Remove the lid and serve.

Nutritional Values per serving:

Calories 101

Total Fat 4.7g

Net Carbs 0.18g

Protein 12.5g

Fiber 0.8g

Cheese Loaded Burgers

Preparation Time: 20 MIN

Serving: 2

Ingredients:

- 1 pound grass-fed lean ground beef
- 1 tbsp. Worcestershire sauce
- ¼ tsp garlic powder
- Salt and freshly ground black pepper, to taste
- 2-ounce shredded cheddar cheese

Directions:

1. In a large bowl, add ground beef, Worcestershire Sauce, garlic powder, salt and black pepper and mix until well combined.
2. Make 4 equal sized balls from the mixture.
3. With your hands, flatten each ball.
4. Place 1-ounce cheese in the center of 2 of the flattened balls.
5. Cover each with remaining 2 flatten balls, pressing the edges together well.
6. In the bottom of Instant Pot, arrange a steamer tray and pour ½ cup of water.
7. Place burgers on top of steamer tray.

8. Secure the lid and place the pressure valve to "Seal" position.
9. Select "Manual" and cook under "High Pressure" for about 5 minutes.
10. Select the "Cancel" and carefully do a "Natural" release.
11. Remove the lid and serve.

Nutritional Values per serving:

Calories 544

Total Fat 23.5g

Net Carbs 1g

Protein 75.9g

Fiber 0g

Mini Sausage Bites

Preparation Time: 20 MIN

Serving: 10

Ingredients:

- 2 pounds gluten-free cut into 1/3-inch thick slices Kielbasa links
- 1 cup sugar-free BBQ sauce
- ½ cup filtered water

Directions:

1. In the bottom of Instant Pot, place all ingredients and stir to combine.
2. Secure the lid and place the pressure valve to "Seal" position.
3. Select "Manual" and cook under "High Pressure" for about 5 minutes.
4. Select the "Cancel" and carefully do a "Natural" release for about 10 minutes and then do a "Quick" release.
5. Remove the lid and transfer the mixture to a serving bowl.
6. Keep aside for about 10-15 minutes before serving.

Nutritional Values per serving:

Calories 243

Total Fat 16g

Net Carbs 1.26g

Protein 11.9g

Fiber 0.2g

Refreshing Curd

Preparation time: 10 minutes

Cooking time: 5 minutes

Servings: 4

Ingredients:

- 3 tablespoons stevia
- 12 ounces raspberries
- 2 egg yolks
- 2 tablespoons lemon juice
- 2 tablespoons ghee

Directions:

1. Put raspberries in your instant pot, add stevia and lemon juice, stir, cover and cook on High for 2 minutes.
2. Strain this into a bowl, add egg yolks, stir well and return to your pot.
3. Set the pot on Simmer mode, cook for 2 minutes, add ghee, stir well, transfer to a container and serve cold.
4. Enjoy!

Nutritional Values per serving: Calories 132, fat 1, fiber 0, carbs 2, protein 4

The Best Jam Ever

Preparation time: 10 minutes

Cooking time: 5 minutes

Servings: 6

Ingredients:

- 4 and ½ cups peaches, peeled and cubed
- 4 tablespoons stevia
- ¼ cup crystallized ginger, chopped

Directions:

1. Set your instant pot on Simmer mode, add peaches, ginger and stevia, stir, bring to a boil, cover and cook on High for 5 minutes.
2. Divide into bowls and serve cold.
3. Enjoy!

Nutritional Values per serving: Calories 53, fat 0, fiber 0, carbs 0, protein 2

Divine Pears

Preparation time: 10 minutes

Cooking time: 4 minutes

Servings: 12

Ingredients:

- 8 pears, cored and cut into quarters
- 1 teaspoon cinnamon powder
- 2 apples, peeled, cored and cut into quarters
- ¼ cup natural apple juice

Directions:

1. In your instant pot, mix pears with apples, cinnamon and apple juice, stir, cover and cook on High for 4 minutes.
2. Blend using an immersion blender, divide into small jars and serve cold
3. Enjoy!

Nutritional Values per serving: Calories 100, fat 0, fiber 0, carbs 0, protein 2

Berry Marmalade

Preparation time: 10 minutes

Cooking time: 20 minutes

Servings: 12

Ingredients:

- 1 pound cranberries
- 1 pound strawberries
- ½ pound blueberries
- ounces black currant
- 4 tablespoons stevia
- Zest from 1 lemon
- A pinch of salt
- 2 tablespoon water

Directions:

1. In your instant pot, mix strawberries with cranberries, blueberries, currants, lemon zest, stevia and water, stir, cover and cook on High for 10 minutes.
2. Divide into jars and serve cold.
3. Enjoy!

Nutritional Values per serving: Calories 87, fat 2, fiber 0, carbs 1, protein 2

Orange Delight

Preparation time: 10 minutes

Cooking time: 25 minutes

Servings: 8

Ingredients:

- Juice from 2 lemons
- 6 tablespoons stevia
- 1 pound oranges, peeled and halved
- 1-pint water

Directions:

1. In your instant pot, mix lemon juice with orange juice and orange segments, water and stevia, cover and cook on High for 15 minutes.
2. Divide into jars and serve cold.

Nutritional Values per serving: Calories 75, fat 0, fiber 0, carbs 2, protein 2

Simple Squash Pie

Preparation time: 10 minutes

Cooking time: 14 minutes

Serving: 8

Ingredients:

- 2 pounds butternut squash, peeled and chopped
- 2 eggs
- 2 cups water
- 1 cup coconut milk
- 2 tablespoons honey
- 1 teaspoon cinnamon powder
- ½ teaspoon ginger powder
- ¼ teaspoon cloves, ground
- 1 tablespoon arrowroot powder
- Chopped pecans

Directions:

1. Put 1 cup water in your instant pot, add the steamer basket, add squash pieces, cover, cook on High for 4 minutes, drain, transfer to a bowl and mash.
2. Add honey, milk, eggs, cinnamon, ginger and cloves, stir very well and pour into ramekins.
3. Add the rest of the water to your instant pot, add the steamer basket, add ramekins inside, cover and cook on High for 10 minutes.
4. Garnish with chopped pecans and serve.
5. Enjoy!

Nutritional Values per serving: Calories 132, fat 1, fiber 2, carbs 2, protein 3

Winter Pudding

Preparation time: 10 minutes

Cooking time: 40 minutes

Servings: 4

Ingredients:

- 4 ounces dried cranberries, soaked for a few hours and drained
- 2 cups water
- 4 ounces apricots, chopped
- 1 cup coconut flour
- 3 teaspoons baking powder
- 3 tablespoons stevia
- 1 teaspoon ginger powder
- A pinch of cinnamon powder
- 15 tablespoons ghee
- 3 tablespoons maple syrup
- 4 eggs
- 1 carrot, grated

Directions:

1. In a blender, mix flour with baking powder, stevia, cinnamon and ginger and pulse a few times.
2. Add ghee, maple syrup, eggs, carrots, cranberries and apricots, stir and spread into a greased pudding pan.
3. Add the water to your instant pot, add the steamer basket, add the pudding, cover and cook on High for 30 minutes.
4. Leave pudding to cool down before serving.
5. Enjoy!

Nutritional Values per serving: Calories 213, fat 2, fiber 1, carbs 3, protein 3

Banana Dessert

Preparation time: 10 minutes

Cooking time: 30 minutes

Servings: 6

Ingredients:

- 2 tablespoons stevia
- 1/3 cup ghee, soft
- 1 teaspoon vanilla
- 1 egg
- 2 bananas, mashed
- 1 teaspoon baking powder
- 1 and ½ cups coconut flour
- ½ teaspoons baking soda
- 1/3 cup coconut milk
- 2 cups water
- Cooking spray

Directions:

1. In a bowl, mix milk stevia, ghee, egg, vanilla and bananas and stir everything.
2. In another bowl, mix flour with salt, baking powder and soda.
3. Combine the 2 mixtures, stir well and pour into a greased cake pan.
4. Add the water to your pot, add the steamer basket, add the cake pan, cover and cook at High for 30 minutes.
5. Leave cake to cool down, slice and serve.
6. Enjoy!

Nutritional Values per serving: Calories 243, fat 1, fiber 1, carbs 2, protein 4

Apple Cake

Preparation time: 10 minutes

Cooking time: 1 hour and 10 minutes

Servings: 6

Ingredients:

- 3 cups apples, cored and cubed
- 1 cup water
- 3 tablespoons stevia
- 1 tablespoon vanilla
- 2 eggs
- 1 tablespoon apple pie spice
- 2 cups coconut flour
- 1 tablespoon baking powder
- 1 tablespoon ghee

Directions:

1. In a bowl mix eggs with ghee, apple pie spice, vanilla, apples and stevia and stir using your mixer.
2. In another bowl, mix baking powder with flour, stir, add to apple mix, stir again well and transfer to a cake pan.
3. Add 1 cup water to your instant pot, add the steamer basket, add cake pan, cover and cook at High for 1 hour and 10 minutes.
4. Cool cake down, slice and serve it.
5. Enjoy!

Nutritional Values per serving: Calories 100, fat 2, fiber 1, carbs 2, protein 2

Special Vanilla Dessert

Preparation time: 10 minutes

Cooking time: 10 minutes

Servings: 4

Ingredients:

- 1 cup almond milk
- 4 tablespoons flax meal
- 2 tablespoons coconut flour
- 2 and ½ cups water
- 2 tablespoons stevia
- 1 teaspoon espresso powder
- 2 teaspoons vanilla extract
- Coconut cream for serving

Directions:

1. In your instant pot, mix flax meal with flour, water, stevia, milk and espresso powder, stir, cover and cook on high for 10 minutes.
2. Add vanilla extract, stir well, leave aside for 5 minutes, divide into bowls and serve with coconut cream on top.
3. Enjoy!

Nutritional Values per serving: Calories 182, fat 2, fiber 1, carbs 3, protein 4

Tasty and Amazing Pear Dessert

Preparation time: 10 minutes

Cooking time: 6 minutes

Servings: 4

Ingredients:

- 1 cup water
- 2 cups pear, peeled and cubed
- 2 cups coconut milk
- 1 tablespoon ghee
- ¼ cups brown stevia
- ½ teaspoon cinnamon powder
- 4 tablespoons flax meal
- ½ cup walnuts, chopped
- ½ cup raisins

Directions:

1. In a heat proof dish, mix milk with stevia, ghee, flax meal, cinnamon, raisins, pears and walnuts and stir.
2. Put the water in your instant pot, add the steamer basket, place heat proof dish inside, cover and cook on High for 6 minutes.
3. Divide this great dessert into small cups and serve cold.
4. Enjoy!

Nutritional Values per serving: Calories 162, fat 3, fiber 1, carbs 2, protein 6

Cranberries Jam

Preparation time: 10 minutes

Cooking time: 15 minutes

Servings: 12

Ingredients:

- 16 ounces cranberries
- 4 ounces raisins
- 3 ounces water+ ¼ cup water
- 8 ounces figs
- 16 ounces strawberries, chopped
- Zest from 1 lemon

Directions:

1. Put figs in your blender, add ¼ cup water, pulse well and strain into a bowl.
2. In your instant pot, mix strawberries with cranberries, lemon zest, raisins, 3 ounces water and figs puree, stir, cover the pot, cook at High for 15 minutes, divide into small jars and serve.

Nutritional Values per serving: Calories 73, fat 1, fiber 1, carbs 2, protein 3

Lemon Jam

Preparation time: 10 minutes

Cooking time: 12 minutes

Servings: 8

Ingredients:

- 2 pounds lemons, sliced
- 2 cups dates
- 1 cup water
- 1 tablespoon vinegar

Directions:

1. Put dates in your blender, add water and pulse really well.
2. Put lemon slices in your instant pot, add dates paste and vinegar, stir, cover and cook on High for 12 minutes.
3. Stir, divide into small jars and serve.
4. Enjoy!

Nutritional Values per serving: Calories 72, fat 2, fiber 1, carbs 2, protein 6

Special Dessert

Preparation time: 10 minutes

Cooking time: 25 minutes

Servings: 4

Ingredients:

- 3 cups rooibos tea
- 1 tablespoon cinnamon, ground
- 2 cups cauliflower, riced
- 2 apples, diced
- 1 teaspoon cloves, ground
- 1 teaspoon turmeric, ground
- A drizzle of honey

Directions:

1. Put cauliflower rice in your instant pot, add tea, stir, cover and cook at High for 10 minutes
2. Add cinnamon, apples, turmeric and cloves, stir, cover and cook at High for 10 minutes mode.
3. Divide into bowls, drizzle honey on top and serve.
4. Enjoy!

Nutritional Values per serving: Calories 152, fat 2, fiber 1, carbs 5, protein 6

Superb Banana Dessert

Preparation time: 10 minutes

Cooking time: 30 minutes

Servings: 4

Ingredients:

- Juice from ½ lemon
- 2 tablespoons stevia
- 3 ounces water
- 1 tablespoon coconut oil
- 4 bananas, peeled and sliced
- ½ teaspoon cardamom seeds

Directions:

1. Put bananas, stevia, water, oil, lemon juice and cardamom in your instant pot, stir a bit, cover and cook on High for 30 minutes, shaking the pot from time to time.
2. Divide into bowls and serve.
3. Enjoy!

Nutritional Values per serving: Calories 87, fat 1, fiber 2, carbs 3, protein 3

Rhubarb Dessert

Preparation time: 10 minutes

Cooking time: 5 minutes

Servings: 4

Ingredients:

- 5 cups rhubarb, chopped
- 2 tablespoons ghee, melted
- 1/3 cup water
- 1 tablespoon stevia
- 1 teaspoon vanilla extract

Directions:

1. Put rhubarb, ghee, water, stevia and vanilla extract in your instant pot, cover and cook on High for 5 minutes.
2. Divide into small bowls and serve cold.
3. Enjoy!

Nutritional Values per serving: Calories 83, fat 2, fiber 1, carbs 2, protein 2

Plum Delight

Preparation time: 10 minutes

Cooking time: 5 minutes

Servings: 10

Ingredients:

- 4 pounds plums, stones removed and chopped
- 1 cup water
- 2 tablespoons stevia
- 1 teaspoon cinnamon, powder
- ½ teaspoon cardamom, ground

Directions:

1. Put plums, water, stevia, cinnamon and cardamom in your instant pot, cover and cook on High for 5 minutes.
2. Stir well, pulse a bit using an immersion blender, divide into small jars and serve.
3. Enjoy!

Nutritional Values per serving: Calories 83, fat 0, fiber 1, carbs 2, protein 5

Refreshing Fruits Dish

Preparation time: 10 minutes

Cooking time: 10 minutes

Servings: 4

Ingredients:

- 1 and ½ pounds plums, stones removed and halved
- 2 tablespoons stevia
- 1 tablespoon cinnamon powder
- 2 apples, cored, peeled and cut into wedges
- 2 tablespoons lemon zest, grated
- 2 teaspoons balsamic vinegar
- 1 cup hot water

Directions:

- Put plums, water, apples, stevia, cinnamon, lemon zest and vinegar in your instant pot, cover and cook on High for 10 minutes.
- Stir again well, divide into small cups and serve cold.

Nutritional Values per serving: Calories 73, fat 0, fiber 1, carbs 2, protein 4

Dessert Stew

Preparation time: 10 minutes

Cooking time: 6 minutes

Servings: 6

Ingredients:

- 14 plums, stones removed and halved
- 2 tablespoons stevia
- 1 teaspoon cinnamon powder
- ¼ cup water
- 2 tablespoons arrowroot powder

Directions:

1. Put plums, stevia, cinnamon, water and arrowroot in your instant pot, cover and cook on High for 6 minutes.
2. Divide into small jars and serve cold.
3. Enjoy!

Nutritional Values per serving: Calories 83, fat 0, fiber 1, carbs 2, protein 2

Original Fruits Dessert

Preparation time: 10 minutes

Cooking time: 10 minutes

Servings: 10

Ingredients:

- 3 cups canned pineapple chunks, drained
- 3 cups canned cherries, drained
- 2 cups canned apricots, halved and drained
- 2 cups canned peach slices, drained
- 3 cups natural applesauce
- 2 cups canned mandarin oranges, drained
- 2 tablespoons stevia
- 1 teaspoon cinnamon powder

Directions:

1. Put pineapples, cherries, apricots, peaches, applesauce, oranges, cinnamon and stevia in your instant pot, cover and cook on High for 10 minutes.
2. Divide into small bowls and serve cold.
3. Enjoy!

Nutritional Values per serving: Calories 120, fat 1, fiber 2, carbs 3, protein 2

Delicious Apples and Cinnamon

Preparation time: 10 minutes

Cooking time: 10 minutes

Servings: 8

Ingredients:

- 1 teaspoon cinnamon powder
- 12 ounces apples, cored and chopped
- 2 tablespoons flax seed meal mixed with 1 tablespoon water
- ½ cup coconut cream
- 3 tablespoons stevia
- ½ teaspoon nutmeg
- 2 teaspoons vanilla extract
- 1/3 cup pecans, chopped

Directions:

1. In your instant pot, mix flax seed meal with coconut cream, vanilla, nutmeg, stevia, apples and cinnamon, stir a bit, cover and cook on High for 10 minutes.
2. Divide into bowls, sprinkle pecans on top and serve.
3. Enjoy!

Nutritional Values per serving: Calories 120, fat 3, fiber 2, carbs 3, protein 3

Crazy Delicious Pudding

Preparation time: 10 minutes

Cooking time: 35 minutes

Servings: 6

Ingredients:

- 1 mandarin, sliced
- Juice from 2 mandarins
- 3 tablespoons stevia
- 4 ounces ghee, melted
- ½ cup water
- 2 tablespoons flax meal
- ¾ cup coconut flour
- 1 teaspoon baking powder
- ¾ cup almonds, ground
- Olive oil cooking spray

Directions:

1. Grease a loaf pan, arrange sliced mandarin on the bottom and leave aside.
2. In a bowl, mix ghee with stevia, flax meal, almonds, mandarin juice, flour and baking powder, stir and spread this over mandarin slices.
3. Add the water to your instant pot, place the trivet on top, add loaf pan, cover and cook on High for 35 minutes.
4. Leave aside to cool down, slice and serve.
5. Enjoy!

Nutritional Values per serving: Calories 200, fat 2, fiber 2, carbs 3, protein 4

Wonderful Berry Pudding

Preparation time: 10 minutes

Cooking time: 35 minutes

Servings: 6

Ingredients:

- 1 cup almond flour
- 2 tablespoons lemon juice
- 2 cups blueberries
- 2 teaspoons baking powder
- ½ teaspoon nutmeg, ground
- ½ cup coconut milk
- 3 tablespoons stevia
- 1 tablespoon flax meal mixed with 1 tablespoon water
- 3 tablespoons ghee, melted
- 1 teaspoon vanilla extract
- 1 tablespoon arrowroot powder
- 1 cup cold water

Directions:

- In a greased heat proof dish, mix blueberries and lemon juice, toss a bit and spread on the bottom.
- In a bowl, mix flour with nutmeg, stevia, baking powder, vanilla, ghee, flaxseed meal, arrowroot and milk, stir well again and spread over blueberries.
- Put the water in your instant pot, add the trivet, and the heatproof dish, cover and cook on High for 35 minutes.
- Leave pudding to cool down, transfer to dessert bowls and serve.
- Enjoy!

Nutritional Values per serving: Calories 220, fat 4, fiber 4, carbs 9, protein 6

Winter Fruits Dessert

Preparation time: 10 minutes

Cooking time: 15 minutes

Servings: 6

Ingredients:

- 1-quart water
- 2 tablespoons stevia
- 1 pound mixed apples, pears and cranberries
- 5-star anise
- A pinch of cloves, ground
- 2 cinnamon sticks
- Zest from 1 orange, grated
- Zest from 1 lemon, grated

Directions:

1. Put the water, stevia, apples, pears, cranberries, star anise, cinnamon, orange and lemon zest and cloves in your instant pot, cover and cook on High for 15 minutes.
2. Serve cold.
3. Enjoy!

Nutritional Values per serving: Calories 98, fat 0, fiber 0, carbs 0, protein 2

Different Dessert

Preparation time: 10 minutes

Cooking time: 4 minutes

Servings: 2

Ingredients:

- 2 cups orange juice
- 4 pears, peeled, cored and cut into medium chunks
- 5 cardamom pods
- 2 tablespoons stevia
- 1 cinnamon stick
- 1 small ginger piece, grated

Directions:

1. Place pears, cardamom, orange juice, stevia, cinnamon and ginger in your instant pot, cover and cook on High for 4 minutes.
2. Divide into small bowls and serve cold.
3. Enjoy!

Nutritional Values per serving: Calories 100, fat 0, fiber 1, carbs 1, protein 2

Orange Dessert

Preparation time: 10 minutes

Cooking time: 30 minutes

Servings: 4

Ingredients:

- 1 and ¾ cup water
- 1 teaspoon baking powder
- 1 cup coconut flour
- 2 tablespoons stevia
- ½ teaspoon cinnamon powder
- 3 tablespoons coconut oil, melted
- ½ cup coconut milk
- ½ cup pecans, chopped
- ½ cup raisins
- ½ cup orange peel, grated
- ¾ cup orange juice

Directions:

1. In a bowl, mix flour with stevia, baking powder, cinnamon, 2 tablespoons oil, milk, pecans and raisins, stir and transfer to a greased heat proof dish.
2. Heat up a small pan over medium high heat, mix ¾ cup water with orange juice, orange peel and the rest of the oil, stir, bring to a boil and pour over the pecans mix.
3. Put 1 cup water in your instant pot, add the trivet, add heat proof dish, cover and cook on High for 30 minutes.
4. Serve cold.
5. Enjoy!

Nutritional Values per serving: Calories 142, fat 3, fiber 1, carbs 3, protein 3

Great Pumpkin Dessert

Preparation time: 10 minutes

Cooking time: 30 minutes

Servings: 10

Ingredients:

- 1 and ½ teaspoons baking powder
- 2 cups coconut flour
- ½ teaspoon baking soda
- ¼ teaspoon nutmeg, ground
- 1 teaspoons cinnamon powder
- ¼ teaspoon ginger, grated
- 1 tablespoon coconut oil, melted
- 1 egg white
- 1 tablespoon vanilla extract
- 1 cup pumpkin puree
- 2 tablespoons stevia
- 1 teaspoon lemon juice
- 1 cup water

Directions:

1. In a bowl, flour with baking powder, baking soda, cinnamon, ginger, nutmeg, oil, egg white, ghee, vanilla extract, pumpkin puree, stevia and lemon juice, stir well and transfer this to a greased cake pan.
2. Put the water in your instant pot, add trivet, add cake pan, cover and cook on High for 30 minutes.
3. Leave cake to cool down, slice and serve.
4. Enjoy!

Nutritional Values per serving: Calories 180, fat 3, fiber 2, carbs 3, protein 4

Delicious Baked Apples

Servings: 6

Cooking Time: 14 minutes

Ingredients:

- 6 apples, cored and cut into wedges
- ¼ tsp nutmeg
- 1 tsp cinnamon
- 1/3 cup honey
- 1 cup red wine
- ¼ cup pecans, chopped
- ¼ cup raisins

Directions:

1. Add all ingredients into the instant pot and stir well.
2. Seal pot with lid and cook on manual mode for 4 minutes.
3. Allow to release pressure naturally for 10 minutes then release using quick release method.
4. Stir well and serve.

Nutritional Values per serving:

Calories: 233; Carbohydrates: 52.7g; Protein: 1g; Fat: 1.3g; Sugar: 42.6g; Sodium: 5mg

Moist Pumpkin Brownie

Servings: 16

Cooking Time: 40 minutes

Ingredients:

- 3 eggs
- 1 tsp pumpkin pie spice
- ¾ cup cocoa powder
- ¼ cup palm sugar
- ¼ cup maple syrup
- ½ cup pumpkin puree
- ¼ cup coconut oil
- Pinch of salt

Directions:

1. Spray baking dish with cooking spray and set aside.
2. Add all ingredients into the large bowl and stir well to combine. Pour batter into the prepared baking dish.
3. Pour 1 cup of water into the instant pot than place trivet in the pot.
4. Place baking dish on top of the trivet.
5. Seal pot with lid and cook on high for 4o minutes.
6. Release pressure using quick release method than open the lid.
7. Remove dish from the pot and set aside to cool completely.
8. Cut into pieces and serve.

Nutritional Values per serving:

Calories: 77; Carbohydrates: 9.3g; Protein: 1.9g; Fat: 4.8g; Sugar: 5.6g; Sodium: 32mg

Lemon Custard

Servings: 4

Cooking Time: 11 minutes

Ingredients:

- 4 eggs
- 1 tsp lemon extract
- 2/3 cup sugar
- 2 tsp lemon zest
- 2 ½ cups milk

Directions:

1. In a saucepan, add lemon zest and milk and heat over medium heat. Bring to boil and stir constantly.
2. Once milk starts to boil up then remove from heat. Set aside to cool for 15 minutes.
3. Pour milk through a strainer into a bowl.
4. In another bowl beat together eggs, lemon extract for 2-3 minutes.
5. Slowly pour milk to the egg mixture and mix until smooth and creamy.
6. Pour mixture into the 4 ramekins and cover each with foil.
7. Pour 2 cups of water into the instant pot than place trivet in the pot.

8. Place ramekins on top of the trivet.
9. Seal pot with lid and cook on high for 8 minutes.
10. Release pressure using quick release method than open the lid.
11. Remove ramekins from the pot and set aside to cool completely.
12. Place custard ramekins in the refrigerator for 2 hours.
13. Serve chilled and enjoy.

Nutritional Values per serving:

Calories: 268; Carbohydrates: 41.5g; Protein: 10.6g; Fat: 7.5g; Sugar: 40.7g; Sodium: 134mg

Pumpkin Pudding

Servings: 4

Cooking Time: 14 minutes

Ingredients:

- 4 cups pumpkin, cubed
- 1 tbsp raisins
- ½ tsp cardamom powder
- ½ cup desiccated coconut
- 10 tbsp brown sugar
- ½ cup almond milk
- 2 tbsp ghee

Directions:

1. Add ghee into the instant pot and set the pot on sauté mode.
2. Add pumpkin and sauté for 2-3 minutes. Add almond milk and stir well.
3. Seal pot with lid and cook on high for 5 minutes.
4. Release pressure using quick release method than open the lid.
5. Mash the pumpkin using the potato masher.
6. Add sugar and cook on sauté mode for 2-3 minutes.
7. Add remaining ingredients and stir well to combine and cook for 2-3 minutes.
8. Serve warm and enjoy.

Nutritional Values per serving:

Calories: 301; Carbohydrates: 14.2g; Protein: 3.5g; Fat: 14.2g; Sugar: 32.3g; Sodium: 23mg

Easy Yogurt Custard

Servings: 6

Cooking Time: 40 minutes

Ingredients:

- 1 cup Greek yogurt
- 2 tsp cardamom powder
- 1 cup milk
- 1 cup condensed milk

Directions:

1. Add all ingredients into the heat-safe bowl and mix until well combined. Cover bowl with foil.
2. Pour 2 cups of water into the instant pot than place trivet in the pot.
3. Place bowl on top of the trivet. Seal pot with lid and cook on high for 20 minutes.
4. Allow to release pressure naturally for 20 minutes then release using quick release method.
5. Remove bowl from the pot and set aside to cool completely.
6. Place custard bowl in refrigerator for 1 hour.
7. Serve chilled and enjoy.

Nutritional Values per serving:

Calories: 215; Carbohydrates: 33.1g; Protein: 7.8g; Fat: 5.8g; Sugar: 32.4g; Sodium: 113mg

Zucchini Pudding

Servings: 4

Cooking Time: 20 minutes

Ingredients:

- 2 cups zucchini, shredded
- ½ tsp cardamom powder
- 1/3 cup sugar
- 5 oz half and half
- 5 oz milk

Directions:

1. Add all ingredients except cardamom to the instant pot and stir well.
2. Seal pot with lid and cook on high for 10 minutes.
3. Allow to release pressure naturally for 10 minutes then release using quick release method.
4. Add cardamom and stir well.
5. Serve and enjoy.

Nutritional Values per serving:

Calories: 136; Carbohydrates: 22g; Protein: 2.9g; Fat: 4.9g; Sugar: 19.3g; Sodium: 37mg

Delicious Pina Colada

Servings: 8

Cooking Time: 12 minutes

Ingredients:

- 1 cup Arborio rice
- 1 tbsp cinnamon
- 5 oz can pineapple, crushed
- oz coconut milk
- 1 cup condensed milk
- 1 ½ cups water

Directions:

1. Add rice and water into the instant pot and stir well.
2. Seal pot with lid and cook on low for 12 minutes.
3. Release pressure using quick release method than open the lid.
4. Add remaining ingredients and stir well.
5. Serve and enjoy.

Nutritional Values per serving:

Calories: 330; Carbohydrates: 45.4g; Protein: 5.8g; Fat: 14.9g; Sugar: 24.2g; Sodium: 59mg

Apple Caramel Cake

Servings: 8

Cooking Time: 35 minutes

Ingredients:

- 21 oz apple fruit filling
- ¼ cup caramel syrup
- ½ cup butter, cut into slices
- 15 oz yellow cake mix

Directions:

1. Spray baking dish with cooking spray. Spread apple fruit filling in the bottom of baking dish.
2. Add caramel syrup and stir to coat.
3. Top with yellow cake mix and butter slices.
4. Pour 1 cup of water into the instant pot than place trivet in the pot.
5. Place baking dish on top of the trivet.
6. Seal pot with lid and cook on high for 35 minutes.
7. Release pressure using quick release method than open the lid.
8. Serve and enjoy.

Nutritional Values per serving:

Calories: 357; Carbohydrates: 57g; Protein: 2g; Fat: 13g; Sugar: 28g; Sodium: 596mg

Apple Rice Pudding

Servings: 8

Cooking Time: 15 minutes

Ingredients:

- ¾ cup Arborio rice
- 1 tsp cinnamon
- 1 cinnamon stick
- 1 tsp vanilla
- ¼ apple, peeled and chopped
- 2 rhubarb stalks, chopped
- ½ cup water
- 1 ½ cup milk

Directions:

1. Add all ingredients into the instant pot and stir well.
2. Seal pot with lid and cook on manual mode for 15 minutes.
3. Release pressure using quick release method than open the lid.
4. Stir well and serve.

Nutritional Values per serving:

Calories: 96; Carbohydrates: 18.3g; Protein: 2.8g; Fat: 1.1g; Sugar: 3g; Sodium: 24mg

Vegan Coconut Risotto Pudding

Servings: 6

Cooking Time: 30 minutes

Ingredients:

- ¾ cup Arborio rice
- ¼ cup maple syrup
- 1 ½ cups water
- ½ cup shredded coconut
- 1 tsp lemon juice
- ½ tsp vanilla
- 15 oz can coconut milk

Directions:

1. Add all ingredients into the instant pot and stir well.
2. Seal pot with lid and cook on manual mode for 20 minutes.
3. Allow to release pressure naturally for 10 minutes then release using quick release method.
4. Stir well and using blender blend pudding until smooth.
5. Serve and enjoy.

Nutritional Values per serving:

Calories: 284; Carbohydrates: 30.8g; Protein: 3.3g; Fat: 17.5g; Sugar: 8.3g; Sodium: 15mg

Vanilla Avocado Pudding

Servings: 2

Cooking Time: 3 minutes

Ingredients:

- 1/2 avocado, cut into cubes
- 1 tsp agar powder
- 1/4 cup coconut cream
- 1 cup coconut milk
- 2 tsp swerve
- 1 tsp vanilla

Directions:

1. Add coconut cream and avocado into the blender and blend until smooth. Set aside.
2. In a large bowl, whisk together coconut milk, vanilla, swerve, and agar powder. Stir until well combined.
3. Add coconut cream and avocado mixture and stir well.
4. Pour mixture into a heat-safe bowl.
5. Pour one cup of water into the instant pot then place a trivet in the pot.
6. Place bowl on top of the trivet.
7. Seal pot with lid and cook on steam mode for 3 minutes.

8. Release pressure using quick release method than open the lid.
9. Remove bowl from the pot and set aside to cool completely.
10. Place bowl in refrigerator for 1 hour.
11. Serve and enjoy.

Nutritional Values per serving:
Calories: 308; Carbohydrates: 27.9g; Protein: 2.1g; Fat: 21.8g; Sugar: 19.6g; Sodium: 32mg

Vanilla Almond Risotto

Servings: 4

Cooking Time: 15 minutes

Ingredients:

- 1 cup Arborio rice
- 1 cup coconut milk
- 2 cups unsweetened almond milk
- 1/4 cup sliced almonds
- 2 tsp vanilla extract
- 1/3 cup sugar

Directions:

1. Add almonds and coconut milk into the instant pot and stir well.
2. Seal pot with lid and cook on high for 5 minutes.
3. Allow to release pressure naturally for 10 minutes then release using quick release method.
4. Stir in vanilla extract and sweetener.
5. Serve and enjoy.

Nutritional Values per serving:

Calories: 432; Carbohydrates: 60.3g; Protein: 6.3g; Fat: 19.3g; Sugar: 19.2g; Sodium: 102mg

Coconut Raspberry Curd

Preparation Time: 20 minutes + chilling time

Servings 4

Nutritional Values per serving: 334 Calories; 32.9g Fat; 6.6g Total Carbs; 2.9g Protein; 3.6g Sugars

Ingredients

- 4 ounces coconut oil, softened
- 3/4 cup Swerve
- 4 egg yolks, beaten
- 1/2 cup blueberries
- 1 teaspoon grated lemon zest
- 1/2 teaspoon vanilla extract
- 1/2 teaspoon star anise, ground

Directions

1. Blend the coconut oil and Swerve in a food processor.
2. Gradually mix in the eggs; continue to blend for 1 minute longer.
3. Now, add blueberries, lemon zest, vanilla, and star anise. Divide the mixture among four Mason jars and cover them with lids.
4. Add 1 ½ cups of water and a metal rack to the Instant Pot. Now, lower your jars onto the rack.

5. Secure the lid. Choose "Manual" mode and High pressure; cook for 15 minutes. Once cooking is complete, use a natural pressure release; carefully remove the lid. Serve
6. Place in your refrigerator until ready to serve. Bon appétit!

Simple Chocolate Mousse

Preparation Time: 20 minutes + chilling time

Servings 6

Nutritional Values per serving: 205 Calories; 18.3g Fat; 5.2g Total Carbs; 3.2g Protein; 2.6g Sugars

Ingredients

- 1 cup full-fat milk
- 1 cup heavy cream
- 4 egg yolks, beaten
- 1/3 cup sugar
- 1/4 teaspoon grated nutmeg
- 1/4 teaspoon ground cinnamon
- 1/4 cup unsweetened cocoa powder

Directions

1. In a small pan, bring the milk and cream to a simmer.
2. In a mixing dish, thoroughly combine the remaining ingredients. Add this egg mixture to the warm milk mixture.
3. Pour the mixture into ramekins.
4. Add 1 ½ cups of water and a metal rack to the Instant Pot. Now, lower your ramekins onto the rack.
5. Secure the lid. Choose "Manual" mode and High pressure; cook for 10 minutes. Once cooking is complete, use a natural pressure release; carefully remove the lid. Serve
6. Serve well chilled and enjoy!

The Best Tropical Dessert Ever

Preparation Time: 15 minutes + chilling time

Servings 4

Nutritional Values per serving: 118 Calories; 8.2g Fat; 6.6g Total Carbs; 3.7g Protein; 2.6g Sugars

Ingredients

- 3 egg yolks, well whisked
- 1/3 cup Swerve
- 1/4 cup water
- 3 tablespoons cacao powder, unsweetened
- 3/4 cup whipping cream
- 1/3 cup coconut milk
- 1/4 cup shredded coconut
- 1 teaspoon vanilla essence
- A pinch of grated nutmeg
- A pinch of salt

Directions

1. Place the egg in a mixing bowl.
2. In a pan, heat the Swerve, water and cacao powder and whisk well to combine.
3. Now, stir in the whipping cream and milk; cook until heated through. Add shredded coconut, vanilla, nutmeg, and salt.
4. Now, slowly and gradually pour the chocolate mixture into the bowl with egg yolks. Stir to combine well and pour into ramekins.
5. Add 1 ½ cups of water and a metal rack to the Instant Pot. Now, lower your ramekins onto the rack.
6. Secure the lid. Choose "Manual" mode and High pressure; cook for 8 minutes. Once cooking is complete, use a quick pressure release; carefully remove the lid.
7. Place in your refrigerator until ready to serve. Bon appétit!

Crème with Almond and Chocolate

Preparation Time: 15 minutes

Servings 4

Nutritional Values per serving: 401 Calories; 37.1g Fat; 5.2g Total Carbs; 9.1g Protein; 1.7g Sugars

Ingredients

- 2 cups heavy whipping cream
- 1/2 cup water
- 4 eggs
- 1/3 cup Swerve
- 1 teaspoon almond extract
- 1 teaspoon vanilla extract
- 1/3 cup almonds, ground
- 2 tablespoons coconut oil, room temperature
- 4 tablespoons cacao powder
- 2 tablespoons gelatin

Directions

1. Start by adding 1 ½ cups of water and a metal rack to your Instant Pot.
2. Blend the cream, water, eggs, Swerve, almond extract, vanilla extract and almonds in your food processor.
3. Add the remaining ingredients and process for a minute longer.
4. Divide the mixture between four Mason jars; cover your jars with lids. Lower the jars onto the rack.
5. Secure the lid. Choose "Manual" mode and High pressure; cook for 7 minutes. Once cooking is complete, use a natural pressure release; carefully remove the lid. Bon appétit!

Cinnamon Flan

Preparation Time: 15 minutes

Servings 6

Nutritional Values per serving: 263 Calories; 21.2g Fat; 3.2g Total Carbs; 10.5g Protein; 2.8g Sugars

Ingredients

- 6 eggs
- 1 cup Swerve
- 1 ½ cups double cream
- 1/2 cup water
- 3 tablespoons dark rum
- A pinch of salt
- A pinch of freshly grated nutmeg
- 1/4 teaspoon ground cinnamon
- 1 teaspoon vanilla extract

Directions

1. Start by adding 1 ½ cups of water and a metal rack to your Instant Pot.
2. In a mixing bowl, thoroughly combine eggs and Swerve. Add double cream, water, rum, salt, nutmeg, cinnamon, and vanilla extract.
3. Pour mixture into a baking dish. Lower the dish onto the rack.
4. Secure the lid. Choose "Manual" mode and High pressure; cook for 10 minutes. Once cooking is complete, use a natural pressure release; carefully remove the lid.
5. Serve well chilled and enjoy!

Yummy Upside-Down Cake

Preparation Time: 35 minutes

Servings 5

Nutritional Values per serving: 193 Calories; 17.9g Fat; 5.1g Total Carbs; 1.2g Protein; 2.4g Sugars

Ingredients

- 1/2 pound raspberries
- 1 ½ tablespoons lemon juice
- 1 cup coconut flour
- 2 tablespoons cassava flour
- 1/2 teaspoon baking powder
- 1/8 teaspoon sea salt
- 1/4 cup coconut oil, melted
- 1 tablespoon monk fruit powder
- 1/2 teaspoon ground cinnamon
- 1/4 teaspoon grated nutmeg
- 1/2 teaspoon orange zest
- 1 teaspoon vanilla paste
- 1 ½ teaspoons powdered agar

Directions

1. Add 1 ½ cups water and a metal rack to the Instant Pot.
2. In a mixing bowl, thoroughly combine raspberries and lemon juice. Spread raspberries in the bottom of the pan.
3. In another mixing bowl, thoroughly combine coconut flour, cassava flour, baking powder, and sea salt.
4. In the third bowl, mix the coconut oil, monk fruit powder, cinnamon, nutmeg, orange zest, and vanilla. Add powdered agar and mix until everything is well incorporated.
5. Pour the liquid ingredients over dry ingredients and mix to form a dough; flatten it to form a circle.
6. Place this dough in a baking pan and cover the raspberries. Cover the pan with a sheet of aluminum foil.
7. Lower the pan onto the metal rack.
8. Secure the lid. Choose "Manual" mode and High pressure; cook for 27 minutes. Once cooking is complete, use a natural pressure release; carefully remove the lid.
9. Finally, turn the cake pan upside down and unmold it on a platter. Enjoy!

Extraordinary Chocolate Cheesecake

Preparation Time: 25 minutes + chilling time

Servings 10

Nutritional Values per serving: 351 Calories; 35.6g Fat; 4.8g Total Carbs; 4.3g Protein; 1.7g Sugars

Ingredients

- Crust:
- 1/3 cup coconut flour
- 1/3 cup almond flour
- 2 tablespoons arrowroot flour
- 2 tablespoons cocoa powder, unsweetened
- 2 tablespoons monk fruit powder
- 1/4 cup coconut oil, melted
- Filling:
- 10 ounces cream cheese, softened
- 8 ounces heavy cream, softened
- 1 teaspoon monk fruit powder
- 1/2 cup cocoa powder, unsweetened
- 3 eggs yolks, at room temperature
- 1/3 cup sour cream
- 4 ounces butter, melted
- 1/2 teaspoon vanilla essence

Directions

1. Prepare your Instant Pot by adding 1 ½ cups of water and a metal rack to its bottom.
2. Coat a bottom of a baking pan with a piece of parchment paper.
3. In mixing bowl, combine coconut flour, almond flour, arrowroot powder, 2 tablespoons of cocoa powder, and 2 tablespoons of monk fruit powder; now, stir in melted coconut oil.
4. Press the crust mixture into the bottom of the prepared baking pan.
5. To make the filling, mix the cream cheese, heavy cream, monk fruit powder, and cocoa powder.
6. Now, fold in the eggs, sour cream, butter, and vanilla; continue to blend until everything is well incorporated,
7. Lower the baking pan onto the rack. Cover with a sheet of foil, making a foil sling.
8. Secure the lid. Choose "Manual" mode and High pressure; cook for 18 minutes. Once cooking is complete, use a natural pressure release; carefully remove the lid.
9. Place this cheesecake in your refrigerator for 3 to 4 hours. Bon appétit!

Old-School Cheesecake

Preparation Time: 35 minutes + chilling time

Servings 10

Nutritional Values per serving: 188 Calories; 17.2g Fat; 4.5g Total Carbs; 5.5g Protein; 1.3g Sugars

Ingredients

- Crust:
- 1/2 cup almond flour
- 1/2 cup coconut flour
- 1 ½ tablespoons powdered erythritol
- 1/4 teaspoon kosher salt
- 3 tablespoons butter, melted
- Filling:
- 8 ounces sour cream, at room temperature
- 8 ounces cream cheese, at room temperature
- 1/2 cup powdered erythritol
- 3 tablespoons orange juice
- 1/2 teaspoon ginger powder
- 1 teaspoon vanilla extract
- 3 eggs, at room temperature

Directions

1. Line a round baking pan with a piece of parchment paper.
2. In a mixing bowl, thoroughly combine all crust ingredients in the order listed above.
3. Press the crust mixture into the bottom of the pan.
4. Then, make the filling by mixing the sour cream and cream cheese until uniform and smooth; add the remaining ingredients and continue to beat until everything is well combined.
5. Pour the cream cheese mixture over the crust. Cover with aluminum foil, making a foil sling.
6. Place 1 ½ cups of water and a metal trivet in your Instant Pot. Then, place the pan on the metal rack.
7. Secure the lid. Choose "Manual" mode and High pressure; cook for 30 minutes. Once cooking is complete, use a natural pressure release; carefully remove the lid. Serve well chilled and enjoy!

Sweet and Sour Tale Cake

Preparation Time: 25 minutes

Servings 6

Nutritional Values per serving: 173 Calories; 15.6g Fat; 2.5g Total Carbs; 6.2g Protein; 1.6g Sugars

Ingredients

- Crust:
- 3/4 cup coconut flour
- 1/4 cup coconut oil
- 2 tablespoons Swerve
- 1/2 teaspoon pure lemon extract
- 1/2 teaspoon pure coconut extract
- 1/2 teaspoon pure vanilla extract
- 1/2 teaspoon baking powder
- A pinch of grated nutmeg
- A pinch of salt
- Filling:
- 4 eggs
- 1/2 cup Swerve
- 3 tablespoons freshly squeezed lemon juice
- 3 tablespoons shredded coconut
- 1/4 teaspoon cinnamon powder

Directions

1. Start by adding 1 ½ cups of water and a metal rack to your Instant Pot. Now, spritz a baking pan with a nonstick cooking spray (butter flavor.
2. Then, thoroughly combine all crust ingredients in your food processor. Now, spread the crust mixture evenly on the bottom of the prepared pan. Do not forget to prick a few holes with a fork.
3. Lower the baking pan onto the rack.
4. Secure the lid. Choose "Manual" mode and High pressure; cook for 8 minutes. Once cooking is complete, use a quick pressure release; carefully remove the lid.
5. Meanwhile, thoroughly combine all filling ingredients in your food processor. Spread the filling mixture evenly over top of the warm crust.
6. Return to the Instant Pot.
7. Secure the lid. Choose "Manual" mode and High pressure; cook for 15 minutes. Once cooking is complete, use a quick pressure release; carefully remove the lid.
8. Cut into squares and serve at room temperature or chilled. Bon appétit!

Lazy Sunday Cake

Preparation Time: 30 minutes

Servings 6

Nutritional Values per serving: 121 Calories; 7.3g Fat; 5.9g Total Carbs; 6.5g Protein; 2.3g Sugars

Ingredients

- 1/2 cup peanut butter
- 1 pound zucchini, shredded
- 1/4 cup Swerve
- 2 eggs, beaten
- 1/2 teaspoon ground star anise
- 1 teaspoon ground cinnamon
- 1/4 teaspoon grated nutmeg
- 1/2 teaspoon rum extract
- 1/2 teaspoon vanilla
- 1/2 teaspoon baking powder

Directions

1. Start by adding 1 ½ cups of water and a metal trivet to your Instant Pot. Now, spritz a baking pan with a nonstick cooking spray.
2. In a mixing dish, thoroughly combine all ingredients until uniform, creamy and smooth. Pour the batter into the prepared pan.
3. Lower the pan onto the trivet.
4. Secure the lid. Choose "Bean/Chili" mode and High pressure; cook for 25 minutes. Once cooking is complete, use a natural pressure release; carefully remove the lid.
5. Allow your cake to cool completely before cutting and serving.Bon appétit!

Keto Chocolate Brownies

Preparation Time: 30 minutes

Servings 6

Nutritional Values per serving: 384 Calories; 36.6g Fat; 5.2g Total Carbs; 7.7g Protein; 1.3g Sugars

Ingredients

- 4 ounces chocolate, sugar-free
- 1/2 cup coconut oil
- 2 cups Swerve
- 4 eggs, whisked
- 1 teaspoon vanilla paste
- 1/4 teaspoon sea salt
- 1/4 teaspoon grated nutmeg
- 1/2 teaspoon dried lavender flowers
- 1/4 cup almond flour
- 1/2 cup whipped cream

Directions

1. Start by adding 1 ½ cups of water and a metal trivet to your Instant Pot. Now, spritz a baking pan with a nonstick cooking spray.
2. Thoroughly combine the chocolate, coconut oil, and Swerve. Gradually, whisk in the eggs. Add the vanilla paste, salt, nutmeg, lavender flowers and almond flour; mix until everything is well incorporated.
3. Secure the lid. Choose "Bean/Chili" mode and High pressure; cook for 25 minutes. Once cooking is complete, use a natural pressure release; carefully remove the lid.
4. Top with whipped cream and serve well chilled. Bon appétit!

Sweet Porridge with a Twist

Preparation Time: 10 minutes

Servings 2

Nutritional Values per serving: 363 Calories; 36.4g Fat; 6.2g Total Carbs; 4.9g Protein; 3.8g Sugars

Ingredients

- 1/2 cup coconut shreds
- 1 tablespoon sunflower seeds
- 2 tablespoons flax seeds
- 2 cardamom pods, crushed slightly
- 1 teaspoon ground cinnamon
- 1 teaspoon Stevia powdered extract
- 1 teaspoon rosewater
- 1/2 cup water
- 1 cup coconut milk

Directions

1. Add all ingredients to the Instant Pot.
2. Secure the lid. Choose "Manual" mode and High pressure; cook for 5 minutes. Once cooking is complete, use a quick pressure release; carefully remove the lid.
3. Ladle into two serving bowls and serve warm. Enjoy!

Cheesecake Tropicana

Preparation Time: 30 minutes + chilling time

Servings 5

Nutritional Values per serving: 268 Calories; 22.7g Fat; 6.6g Total Carbs; 9.5g Protein; 4.2g Sugars

Ingredients

- 9 ounces cream cheese
- 1/3 cup Swerve
- 1/2 teaspoon ginger powder
- 1 teaspoon grated orange zest
- 1 teaspoon vanilla extract
- 3 eggs
- 4 tablespoons double cream
- 1 tablespoon Swerve
- 1 navel orange, peeled and sliced

Directions

1. Start by adding 1 ½ cups of water and a metal rack to your Instant Pot. Now, spritz a baking pan with a nonstick cooking spray.
2. Beat cream cheese, 1/3 cup of Swerve, ginger, grated orange zest, and vanilla with an electric mixer.
3. Now, gradually fold in the eggs, and continue to mix until everything is well incorporated. Press this

mixture into the prepared baking pan and cover with foil.
4. Secure the lid. Choose "Bean/Chili" mode and High pressure; cook for 25 minutes. Once cooking is complete, use a natural pressure release; carefully remove the lid.
5. Mix the cream and 1 tablespoon of Swerve; spread this topping on the cake. Allow it to cool on a wire rack.
6. Then, transfer your cake to the refrigerator. Garnish with orange slices and serve well chilled. Bon appétit!

Classic Holiday Custard

Preparation Time: 20 minutes + chilling time

Servings 4

Nutritional Values per serving: 201 Calories; 17.7g Fat; 6.2g Total Carbs; 4.2g Protein; 1.2g Sugars

Ingredients

- 5 egg yolks
- 1/3 cup coconut milk, unsweetened
- 1/2 teaspoon vanilla extract
- 1 teaspoon monk fruit powder
- 1 tablespoon butterscotch flavoring
- 1/2 stick butter, melted

Directions

1. Blend the egg yolks with coconut milk, vanilla extract, monk fruit powder, and butterscotch flavoring.
2. Then, stir in the butter; stir until everything is well incorporated. Divide the mixture among four Mason jars and cover them with lids.
3. Add 1 ½ cups of water and a metal rack to the Instant Pot. Now, lower your jars onto the rack.
4. Secure the lid. Choose "Manual" mode and Low pressure; cook for 15 minutes. Once cooking is complete, use a natural pressure release; carefully remove the lid. Serve
5. Place in your refrigerator until ready to serve. Bon appétit!

Blackberry Espresso Brownies

Preparation Time: 30 minutes

Servings 8

Nutritional Values per serving: 151 Calories; 13.6g Fat; 6.7g Total Carbs; 4.1g Protein; 1.1g Sugars

Ingredients

- 4 eggs
- 1 ¼ cups coconut cream
- 1 teaspoon Stevia liquid concentrate
- 1/3 cup cocoa powder, unsweetened
- 1/2 teaspoon grated nutmeg
- 1/2 teaspoon cinnamon powder
- 1 teaspoon espresso coffee
- 1 teaspoon pure almond extract
- 1 teaspoon pure vanilla extract
- 1 teaspoon baking powder
- A pinch of kosher salt
- 1 cup blackberries, fresh or frozen (thawed

Instructions

1. Start by adding 1 ½ cups of water and a metal rack to your Instant Pot. Now, spritz a baking pan with a nonstick cooking spray.

2. Now, mix eggs, coconut cream, Stevia, cocoa powder, nutmeg, cinnamon, coffee, pure almond extract vanilla, baking powder, and salt with an electric mixer.
3. Crush the blackberries with a fork. After that, fold in your blackberries into the prepared mixture.
4. Pour the batter into the prepared pan.
5. Secure the lid. Choose "Bean/Chili" mode and High pressure; cook for 25 minutes. Once cooking is complete, use a natural pressure release; carefully remove the lid. Bon appétit!

Sweet Porridge with Blueberries

Preparation Time: 10 minutes

Servings 4

Nutritional Values per serving: 219 Calories; 18.2g Fat; 6.2g Total Carbs; 5.6g Protein; 2.9g Sugars

Ingredients

- 6 tablespoons golden flax meal
- 6 tablespoons coconut flour
- 2 cups water
- 1/4 teaspoon freshly grated nutmeg
- 1/4 teaspoon Himalayan salt
- 3 egg, whisked
- 1/2 stick butter, softened
- 4 tablespoons double cream
- 4 tablespoons monk fruit powder
- 1 cup blueberries

Directions

1. Add all ingredients to the Instant Pot.
2. Secure the lid. Choose "Manual" mode and High pressure; cook for 5 minutes. Once cooking is complete, use a quick pressure release; carefully remove the lid.
3. Serve garnished with some extra berries if desired. Enjoy!

Vanilla Berry Cupcakes

Preparation Time: 35 minutes

Servings 6

Nutritional Values per serving: 403 Calories; 42.1g Fat; 4.1g Total Carbs; 4.2g Protein; 2.1g Sugars

Ingredients

- Cupcakes:
- 1/2 cup coconut flour
- 1/2 cup almond flour
- 1/2 teaspoon baking soda
- 1 teaspoon baking powder
- A pinch of salt
- A pinch of grated nutmeg
- 1 teaspoon ginger powder
- 1 stick butter, at room temperature
- 1/2 cup Swerve
- 3 eggs, beaten
- 1/2 teaspoon pure coconut extract
- 1/2 teaspoon pure vanilla extract
- 1/2 cup double cream
- Frosting:
- 1 stick butter, at room temperature
- 1/2 cup Swerve

- 1 teaspoon pure vanilla extract
- 1/2 teaspoon coconut extract
- 6 tablespoons coconut, shredded
- 3 tablespoons raspberry, puréed
- 6 frozen raspberries

Directions

1. Start by adding 1 ½ cups of water and a rack to your Instant Pot.
2. In a mixing dish, thoroughly combine the cupcake ingredients. Divide the batter between silicone cupcake liners. Cover with a piece of foil.
3. Place the cupcakes on the rack.
4. Secure the lid. Choose "Manual" mode and High pressure; cook for 25 minutes. Once cooking is complete, use a natural pressure release; carefully remove the lid.
5. In the meantime, thoroughly combine the frosting ingredients. Put this mixture into a piping bag and top your cupcakes.
6. Garnish with frozen raspberries and enjoy!

Mini Cheesecakes with Berries

Preparation Time: 25 minutes

Servings 6

Nutritional Values per serving: 232 Calories; 22.1g Fat; 4.8g Total Carbs; 5.7g Protein; 1.9g Sugars

Ingredients

- 1/4 cup sesame seed flour
- 1/4 cup hazelnut flour
- 1/2 cup coconut flour
- 1 ½ teaspoons baking powder
- A pinch of kosher salt
- A pinch of freshly grated nutmeg
- 1/2 teaspoon ground star anise
- 1/2 teaspoon ground cinnamon
- 1/2 stick butter
- 1 cup Swerve
- 2 eggs, beaten
- 1/2 cup cream cheese
- 1/3 cup fresh mixed berries
- 1/2 vanilla paste

Directions

1. Start by adding 1 ½ cups of water and a rack to your Instant Pot.
2. In a mixing dish, thoroughly combine all of the above ingredients. Divide the batter between lightly greased ramekins. Cover with a piece of foil.
3. Place the ramekins on the rack.
4. Secure the lid. Choose "Manual" mode and High pressure; cook for 20 minutes. Once cooking is complete, use a natural pressure release; carefully remove the lid.

Special Berry Crisp with Cinnamon

Preparation Time: 15 minutes

Servings 4

Nutritional Values per serving: 255 Calories; 24.6g Fat; 5.6g Total Carbs; 3.4g Protein; 2.5g Sugars

Ingredients

- 1/2 pound blackberries
- 1 teaspoon ground cinnamon
- 1/4 teaspoon grated nutmeg
- 1/2 teaspoon ground cardamom
- 1/2 teaspoon vanilla paste
- 1/2 cup water
- 1/4 cup Swerve
- 5 tablespoons coconut oil, melted
- 1/2 cup almonds, roughly chopped
- 1/4 cup coconut flour
- 1/4 teaspoon Stevia
- A pinch of salt

Directions

1. Place blackberries on the bottom of your Instant Pot. Sprinkle with cinnamon, nutmeg, and cardamom. Add vanilla, water and Swerve.
2. In a mixing bowl, thoroughly combine the remaining ingredients. Drop by the spoonful on top of the blackberries.
3. Secure the lid. Choose "Manual" mode and High pressure; cook for 10 minutes. Once cooking is complete, use a natural pressure release; carefully remove the lid.
4. Serve at room temperature and enjoy!

Yummy Fire Cheesecake

Preparation Time: 40 minutes

Servings 6

Nutritional Values per serving: 373 Calories; 36.7g Fat; 5.1g Total Carbs; 8g Protein; 2.6g Sugars

Ingredients

- 1/2 cup almond flour
- 1/2 cup coconut flour
- 4 tablespoons coconut oil, melted
- 3/4 pound cream cheese, at room temperature
- 3/4 cup Swerve
- 3 eggs
- A pinch of salt
- A pinch of grated nutmeg
- 1/2 teaspoon ground cinnamon
- 1/2 teaspoon ground star anise
- 1 teaspoon vanilla extract
- 1 teaspoon red food coloring

Directions

1. Start by adding 1 ½ cups of water and a metal rack to your Instant Pot.

2. In a mixing bowl, thoroughly combine almond flour, coconut flour, and coconut oil. Press this mixture into a lightly greased cheesecake pan.
3. In another mixing bowl, beat the cream cheese together with Swerve. Fold in the eggs, one at a time, and continue to beat until well mixed.
4. Then, add the spices and extract; mix until everything is well incorporated. Spread the filling over the top of your cheesecake. Lower the pan onto the rack.
5. Secure the lid. Choose "Bean/Chili" mode and High pressure; cook for 35 minutes. Once cooking is complete, use a natural pressure release; carefully remove the lid. Bon appétit!

Classic Carrot Cake

Preparation Time: 35 minutes

Servings 8

Nutritional Values per serving: 381 Calories; 35.1g Fat; 4.4g Total Carbs; 10.3g Protein; 1.7g Sugars

Ingredients

- Carrot Cake:
- 2 cups carrots, grated
- 1 cup almond flour
- 1/2 cup coconut, shredded
- 1/4 cup hazelnuts, chopped
- 1/4 teaspoon ground cloves
- 1/4 teaspoon grated nutmeg
- 1/2 teaspoon ground cinnamon
- 1/2 teaspoon baking soda
- 1 teaspoon baking powder
- 4 tablespoons Swerve
- 1 teaspoon pure vanilla extract
- 4 eggs, beaten
- 1 stick butter, melted
- Cream Cheese Frosting:

1 cup cream cheese

2 tablespoons Swerve

1/2 teaspoon pure vanilla extract

Directions

1. Start by adding 1 ½ cups of water and a metal rack to your Instant Pot. Now, spritz a cheesecake pan with a nonstick cooking spray.
2. In a mixing bowl, thoroughly combine dry ingredients for the cake. Then, mix the wet ingredients until everything is well combined.
3. Pour the wet mixture into the dry mixture and stir to combine well. Spoon the batter into the cheesecake pan.
4. Cover with a sheet of foil. Lower the pan onto the rack.
5. Secure the lid. Choose "Bean/Chili" mode and High pressure; cook for 30 minutes. Once cooking is complete, use a quick pressure release; carefully remove the lid.
6. Meanwhile, mix the frosting ingredients. Frost the carrot cake and serve chilled. Enjoy!

Classic Brownie with Blackberry-Goat Cheese Swirl

Preparation Time: 30 minutes

Servings 8

Nutritional Values per serving: 309 Calories; 27.6g Fat; 3.4g Total Carbs; 10.8g Protein; 1.1g Sugars

Ingredients

- Brownies:
- 5 tablespoons coconut oil, melted
- 1 cup Swerve
- 1/4 cup cocoa powder, unsweetened
- 3 teaspoons water
- 1/2 teaspoon vanilla extract
- 3 eggs, beaten
- 1/4 cup golden flax meal
- 3/4 cup almond flour
- 1/2 teaspoon baking soda
- 1/2 teaspoon baking powder
- A pinch of salt
- A pinch of grated nutmeg
- 1/4 cup chocolate chunks, sugar-free

Blackberry Goat Cheese Swirl:

- 2 tablespoons unsalted butter, softened
- 4 ounces goat cheese, softened
- 2 ounces cream cheese, softened
- 1 cup blackberries, fresh or frozen (thawed
- 1 tablespoon Swerve
- 1/2 teaspoon almond extract
- A pinch of salt

Directions

1. Start by adding 1 ½ cups of water and a metal rack to your Instant Pot. Now, spritz a square cake pan with a nonstick cooking spray.
2. Mix the coconut oil with Swerve, cocoa powder, water, and vanilla until well combined. Mix in the eggs, flour, baking soda, baking powder, salt, and nutmeg.
3. Mix until smooth and creamy. Add the chocolate and mix one more time. Add the batter to the prepared pan.
4. Secure the lid. Choose "Manual" mode and High pressure; cook for 25 minutes. Once cooking is complete, use a quick pressure release; carefully remove the lid.
5. Invert your brownie onto a platter. Allow it to cool to room temperature.

6. Meanwhile, make the blackberry-goat cheese swirl. Beat the butter and cheese with an electric mixer; add blackberries, Swerve, almond extract and salt and continue to beat until light and fluffy.
7. Drop this mixture on top of your brownie in spoonfuls; then swirl it with a knife. Bon appétit!

Special Birthday Cake

Preparation Time: 35 minutes + chilling time

Servings 8

Nutritional Values per serving: 230 Calories; 18.8g Fat; 6.1g Total Carbs; 8.9g Protein; 1.4g Sugars

Ingredients

- Batter:
- 1 cup hazelnut flour
- 2 tablespoons arrowroot starch
- 1/2 cup cocoa powder
- 1 ¼ teaspoons baking powder
- 1/4 teaspoon kosher salt
- 1/4 teaspoon freshly grated nutmeg
- 6 eggs, whisked
- 8 tablespoons coconut oil, melted
- 1 teaspoon pure vanilla extract
- 1/2 teaspoon pure hazelnut extract
- 2/3 cup Swerve
- 1/3 cup full-fat milk
- Hazelnut Ganache:
- 1/2 cup heavy cream
- 5 ounces dark chocolate, sugar-free
- 2 tablespoons coconut oil

Directions

1. Start by adding 1 ½ cups of water and a metal rack to your Instant Pot. Now, lightly grease a baking pan with a nonstick cooking spray.
2. In a mixing bowl, thoroughly combine dry ingredients for the batter. In another bowl, mix wet ingredients for the batter.
3. Add wet mixture to the dry mixture; mix to combine well. Pour the mixture into the prepared baking pan.
4. Secure the lid. Choose "Bean/Chili" mode and High pressure; cook for 30 minutes. Once cooking is complete, use a natural pressure release; carefully remove the lid.
5. Now, place the cake pan on a wire rack until it is cool to the touch. Allow it to cool completely before frosting.
6. Meanwhile, make your ganache. In a medium pan, bring the heavy cream to a boil. Turn the heat off as soon as you see the bubbles.
7. Add chocolate and coconut oil and whisk to combine well. Frost the cake and serve well chilled.

Holiday Blueberry Pudding

Preparation Time: 20 minutes

Servings 6

Nutritional Values per serving:240 Calories; 20.5g Fat; 5.4g Total Carbs; 4.8g Protein; 3.1g Sugars

Ingredients

- 1 cup almond flour
- 3 tablespoons sunflower seed flour
- 1/2 cup Swerve
- 1/2 teaspoon baking soda
- 1 teaspoon baking powder
- 1/4 cup coconut cream
- 1/4 cup water
- 1/4 cup coconut oil, softened
- 2 tablespoons dark rum
- 1/2 teaspoon vanilla
- 1/2 cup blueberries

Directions

1. Start by adding 1 ½ cups of water and a metal trivet to your Instant Pot.
2. Mix all ingredients, except blueberries, until everything is well incorporated. Spoon the mixture into a lightly greased baking pan.

3. Fold in blueberries and gently stir to combine. Lower the baking dish onto the trivet.
4. Secure the lid. Choose "Bean/Chili" mode and High pressure; cook for 15 minutes. Once cooking is complete, use a natural pressure release; carefully remove the lid.
5. Allow the cobbler to cool slightly before serving. Bon appétit!

Fluffy Strawberry Cake

Preparation Time: 35 MIN

Serving: 6

Ingredients:

- 2 cups almond flour
- 1 cup coconut flour
- ¼ cup unsweetened cocoa powder
- 1 tsp baking soda
- ½ tsp baking powder
- ½ tsp salt
- 1 cup unsweetened almond milk
- 3 eggs
- 2 egg whites
- 3 cups whipped cream, sugar-free
- 1 tsp stevia extract
- 2 tsp strawberry extract

Directions:

1. Line a 7-inches springform pan with some parchment paper. Set aside.
2. In a large mixing bowl, combine almond flour, coconut flour, cocoa powder, baking soda, baking powder, and salt. Mix well and gradually add milk. With a paddle attachment on, beat well on high speed. Now add eggs,

one at the time, beating constantly. Finally, add egg whites and mix until completely incorporated. Transfer the mixture to the prepared springform pan and flatten the surface with a kitchen spatula. Cover loosely with some aluminum foil.
3. Plug in your Instant Pot and pour in 1 cup of water. Set the trivet in the stainless steel insert and gently place the springform on top.
4. Seal the lid and set the steam release handle to the 'Sealing' position. Press the 'Manual' button and set the timer for 20 minutes.
5. When done, move the steam valve to the 'Venting' position to release the pressure.
6. Open the lid and carefully remove the springform pan. Place on a wire rack and cool to a room temperature.
7. Meanwhile, place whipped cream, stevia, and strawberry extract in a large bowl. Using a hand mixer, beat well until fully combined.
8. Pour the mixture over the chilled crust and refrigerate for one hour before use.

Nutritional Values per serving:

Calories 195

Total Fats 16.4g

Net Carbs: 4.2g

Protein 5.7g

Fiber: 3.8g

Chocolate Cheesecake

Preparation Time: 45 MIN

Serving: 10

Ingredients:

- 1 cup almond flour
- 1 cup coconut flour
- 1 cup unsweetened cocoa powder, divided in half
- ¼ cup swerve
- ½ cup butter
- 2 large eggs
- 4 cups cream cheese
- ¾ cup heavy cream
- 1 tsp vanilla extract
- ½ tsp stevia powder
- 2 tbsp. oil

Directions:

1. In a large bowl, combine together almond flour, coconut flour, unsweetened cocoa powder, and swerve. Mix well and transfer to a food processor along with butter and eggs. Process well and set aside.
2. Brush a 7-inches springform pan with oil and line with some parchment paper. Add the crust mixture and press well with your hands.

3. Plug in your instant pot and pour into 1 ½ cups of water. Place the trivet in the stainless steel insert and gently put the springform on top. Cover with some aluminum foil to prevent condensate dripping.
4. Seal the lid and set the steam release handle to 'Sealing' position. Press the 'Manual' button and set the timer for 15 minutes.
5. When you hear the cooker's end signal, release the pressure naturally for 10-12 minutes. Move the pressure valve to the 'Venting' position to release any remaining pressure.
6. Open the lid and gently remove the springform pan. Chill to a room temperature.
7. Place cream cheese, heavy cream, vanilla extract, and stevia powder in a blender. Pulse to combine and pour the mixture over the chilled crust.
8. Refrigerate overnight.

Nutritional Values per serving:

Calories 548

Total Fats 52g

Net Carbs: 7.4g

Protein 12g

Fiber: 6.8g

Raspberry Compote

Preparation Time: 45 MIN

Serving: 4

Ingredients:

- 2 cups raspberries
- 1 cup swerve
- 1 tsp freshly grated lemon zest
- 1 tsp vanilla extract

Directions:

1. Plug in your instant pot and press the 'Saute' button. Add raspberries, swerve, lemon zest, and vanilla extract. Stir well and pour in 1 cup of water. Cook for 5 minutes, stirring constantly.
2. Now pour in 2 more cups of water and press the 'Cancel' button. Seal the lid and set the steam release handle to the 'Sealing' position. Press the 'Manual' button and set the timer for 15 minutes on low pressure.
3. When you hear the cooker's end signal, press the 'Cancel' button and release the pressure naturally for 10-15 minutes. Move the pressure handle to the 'Venting' position to release any remaining pressure and open the lid.

4. Optionally, stir some more lemon juice and transfer to serving bowls.
5. Chill to a room temperature and refrigerate for one hour before serving.

Nutritional Values per serving:

Calories 48

Total Fats 0.5g

Net Carbs: 5g

Protein 1g

Fiber: 5.3g

Chocolate Cream

Preparation Time: 25 MIN

Serving: 4

Ingredients:

- 2 heavy cream
- ¼ cup unsweetened dark chocolate, chopped
- 3 eggs
- 1 tsp orange zest
- 1 tsp stevia powder
- 1 tsp vanilla extract
- ½ tsp salt

Directions:

1. Plug in your instant pot and press the 'Saute' button. Add heavy cream, chopped chocolate, stevia powder, vanilla extract, orange zest, and salt. Stir well and simmer until the chocolate has completely melted. Press the 'Cancel' button and crack eggs, one at the time, stirring constantly. Remove from the instant pot.
2. Transfer the mixture to 4 mason jars with loose lids.
3. Pour 2 cups of water in your instant pot and set the trivet in the stainless steel insert. Add jars and seal the lid.

4. Set the steam release handle and press the 'Manual' button. Set the timer for 10 minutes.
5. When done, perform a quick release by moving the steam valve to the 'Venting' position.
6. Open the lid and remove the jars. Chill to a room temperature and then transfer to the refrigerator.
7. Top with some whipped cream before serving.

Nutritional Values per serving:

Calories 267

Total Fats 26.2g

Net Carbs: 2.4g

Protein 5.6g

Fiber: 0.2g

Butter Pancakes

Preparation Time: 15 MIN

Serving: 6

Ingredients:

- 2 cups cream cheese
- 2 cups almond flour
- 6 large eggs
- ¼ tsp salt
- 2 tbsp. butter
- ¼ tsp ground ginger
- ½ tsp cinnamon powder

Directions:

1. In a large mixing bowl, combine cream cheese, eggs, and one tablespoon of butter. With a paddle attachment on, beat well on high speed until light and creamy. Slowly add flour beating constantly. Finally, add salt, ginger, and cinnamon. Continue to beat until fully incorporated.
2. Plug in your instant pot and press the 'Saute' button. Grease the stainless steel insert with the remaining butter and heat up.

3. Pour in about ½ cup of the batter and cook for 2-3 minutes or until golden color. Repeat the process with the remaining batter.
4. Serve warm.

Nutritional Values per serving:

Calories 432

Total Fats 40.2g

Net Carbs: 3.5g

Protein 14.2g

Fiber: 1g

Lemon Cupcakes with Blueberries

Preparation Time: 35 MIN

Serving: 6

Ingredients:

- 2 cups almond flour
- 2/3 tsp baking powder
- ¼ tsp baking soda
- ½ tsp xanthan gum
- 1 cup swerve
- 3 eggs
- 1 cup almond milk, unsweetened
- ¼ cup blueberries
- 1 tbsp. butter, softened
- 1 tbsp. coconut oil
- 1 tbsp. lemon zest, freshly grated
- 1 tsp vanilla extract

Directions:

1. Combine all dry ingredients in a large mixing bowl. Mix well and gradually add milk. Beat well on medium speed adding eggs, one at the time. Add butter, coconut oil, lemon zest, and vanilla extract. Mix until fully incorporated. Fold in blueberries and transfer to 12-cup silicone cupcake pan.

2. Plug in your instant pot and pour in 1 cup of water. Set the trivet in the stainless steel insert and place the silicone pan on top. Cover loosely with some aluminum foil and seal the lid.
3. Set the steam release handle to the 'Sealing' position and press the 'Manual' button. Set the timer for 25 minutes.
4. When done, perform a quick pressure release and open the lid. Gently remove the muffin pan from your instant pot and cool completely before serving.

Nutritional Values per serving:

Calories 223

Total Fats 20.4g

Net Carbs: 3.8g

Protein 5.9g

Fiber: 2.9g

Chocolate Brownies

Preparation Time: 30 MIN

Serving: 8

Ingredients:

- ½ cup cocoa powder, unsweetened
- ¼ cup unsweetened dark chocolate chunks
- 1 cup cream cheese
- 2 large eggs
- 3 tbsp. coconut oil
- ½ tsp salt
- ¾ cup swerve

Directions:

1. Combine cream cheese, eggs, and coconut oil in a large mixing bowl. With a paddle attachment on, beat well on medium speed until smooth. Add cocoa powder, salt, swerve, and dark chocolate chunks. Continue to beat for 2 minutes, or until fully incorporated.
2. Brush a 7-inches cake pan with some oil and line with some parchment paper. Dust the paper with some cocoa powder and pour in the batter. Flatten the surface with a kitchen spatula and loosely cover with aluminum foil.

3. Plug in your instant pot and pour in 1 cup of water. Set the steam rack at the bottom of the steel insert and place the cake pan on top.
4. Seal the lid and set the steam release to the 'Sealing' position. Select the 'Manual' mode and set the timer for 20 minutes.
5. When you hear the cooker's end signal, release the pressure naturally for 15 minutes. Open the lid and carefully remove the pan.
6. Cool completely and cut into 8 brownies.

Nutritional Values per serving:

Calories 180

Total Fats 17.5g

Net Carbs: 2.4g

Protein 4.8g

Fiber: 1.7g

Peach Pie

Preparation Time: 40 MIN

Serving: 6

Ingredients:

- 2 cups almond flour
- 1 medium-sized peach, sliced
- ¼ cup raspberries
- 4 large eggs
- 6 tbsp. butter
- 2 tsp baking powder
- ½ tsp salt
- ¼ cup swerve
- ¼ tsp vanilla extract
- 2 tsp lemon zest

Directions:

1. Brush a 7-inches cake pan with oil and line with some parchment paper. Set aside.
2. In a medium-sized bowl, whisk together eggs and swerve. Set aside.
3. In another bowl, combine all the remaining dry ingredients and mix well. Slowly pour in the egg mixture, mixing constantly, and add the remaining

ingredients. Transfer to a mixing bowl and beat for 2 minutes on medium speed.
4. Pour the mixture into the prepared cake pan and shake a couple of times to flatten the surface. Wrap with some aluminum foil.
5. Plug in your instant pot and pour in 1 cup of water. Set the trivet at the bottom of the stainless steel insert and place the wrapped pan on top. Seal the lid and set the steam release handle to the 'Sealing' position.
6. Select the 'Manual' mode and set the timer for 25 minutes.
7. When done, perform a quick release by moving the pressure valve to the 'Venting' position.
8. Open the lid and remove the pan. Cool completely before serving.

Nutritional Values per serving:

Calories 221

Total Fats 19.4g

Net Carbs: 4.4g

Protein 6.6g

Fiber: 1.8g

Almond Butter Cookies

Preparation Time: 40 MIN

Serving: 15

Ingredients:

- 1 ½ cup almond flour
- ½ cup coconut flour
- 3 eggs
- ¾ cup coconut oil, melted
- 3 tbsp. almond butter
- ¼ cup cocoa powder, unsweetened
- ½ cup swerve
- ½ tsp salt

Directions:

1. Plug in your instant pot and pour in 1 cup of water. Set the trivet at the bottom of the stainless steel insert and set aside.
2. Line a round baking pan with some parchment paper and set aside.
3. In a large mixing bowl, combine together almond flour, coconut flour, cocoa butter, swerve, and salt. Add eggs, coconut oil, and almond butter. With a paddle attachment on, beat well on high speed until fully incorporated.

4. Scoop out 15 cookies and place them in the prepared baking pan. You will probably have to do this in several batches. Gently flatten each cookie with the palm of your hand and place the pan in your instant pot. Cover with aluminum foil.
5. Seal the lid and set the steam release handle. Press the 'Manual' button and set the timer for 25 minutes.
6. When done, release the pressure naturally for 15 minutes. Move the pressure handle to the 'Venting' position to release any remaining pressure.
7. Open the lid and remove the pan. Cool to a room temperature and then transfer the cookies to a wire rack to cool completely.

Nutritional Values per serving:

Calories 154

Total Fats 15.3g

Net Carbs: 1.5g

Protein 2.9g

Fiber: 1.9g

Mini Brownie Cakes

Preparation Time: 25 MIN

Serving: 4

Ingredients:

- 1 cup almond flour
- ½ cup cocoa powder, unsweetened
- ¼ cup swerve
- 4 eggs
- ¼ cup unsweetened dark chocolate, cut into chunks
- 1 tsp rum extract
- ½ cup coconut oil

Directions:

1. Plug in your instant pot and pour in 1 cup of water. Set the trivet at the bottom of the stainless steel insert and set aside.
2. In a large mixing bowl, combine together eggs, swerve, dark chocolate chunks, rum extract, and coconut oil. Mix well until light and creamy mixture. Sift almond flour and cocoa powder over the egg mixture and mix well again.
3. Divide the mixture between 4 ramekins and tightly wrap with aluminum foil. Place each ramekin on the trivet and seal the lid.

4. Set the steam release handle to the 'Sealing' position. Press the 'Manual' button and set the timer for 15 minutes.
5. When done, release the pressure naturally for another 15 minutes.
6. Open the lid and gently remove the ramekins using oven mitts. Place on a wire rack and cool completely before serving.

Nutritional Values per serving:

Calories 404

Total Fats 39.1g

Net Carbs: 4.8g

Protein 9.7g

Fiber: 4.7g

www.ingramcontent.com/pod-product-compliance
Lightning Source LLC
Chambersburg PA
CBHW070420120526
44590CB00014B/1474